MY TRUE LOVE FOR FARMING

MY TRUE LOVE FOR FARMING

Chris Brettell

Library of Congress Control Number:		2020903586
ISBN:	Hardcover	978-1-9845-9407-5
	Softcover	978-1-9845-9406-8
	eBook	978-1-9845-9405-1

Print information available on the last page.

Rev. date: 05/12/2020

To order additional copies of this book, contact:
Xlibris
800-056-3182
www.Xlibrispublishing.co.uk
Orders@Xlibrispublishing.co.uk
791306

CONTENTS

DEDICATION

For my wife Soraya, sister Christine, brother Charles, my children Kevin, Karen and Nicola and grandchildren Oliver, Abbie, Jacob, Samuel and Isaac, along with nieces and nephews Marissa, Cameron, Barclay, Mindy, Sharon, Sarah and Paul. And Heidi the dog.

Christopher: From the Greek meaning 'Christ-bearer'. He is strong, handsome and intelligent and sets a good example to others. A man you can rely on.

1944-50

I was born at 23 Frances Road, Hounslow, Middlesex, London in 1944. Life started for me towards the end of World War II. My Father was a Major in the army and came out of the services in 1948. By this time, I was four years old and I can just about remember the move we made from Hounslow. In those days you hardly ever saw any cars, only horses and carts. I also remember the trams running in London and I loved travelling on them as often as I could. We only lived in Hounslow for about a year or two and moved to a bungalow called Kedge Anchor in Fryer Road, Wraysbury, Berkshire. I used to love watching the tiddlers from our boat landing stage. We overlooked the River Thames and could see Windsor Castle. Such fond memories. When we wanted to get to the Windsor town side, we were able to cross the river by rowing boat. As a child I also remember the day tripper boats which sailed down the River Thames. I loved the idea of being on a big boat. Luckily the river boats were still there for me when I was much older and it felt good to take my own children on them, and many times since. They still run today.

Young Geoffrey, Brian, Chris and Mother

Father, Alfred Brettell

Alfred Brettell Leading Marching Soldiers

First School in Wraysbury

In April 1949, I started school in Wraysbury village; it was about two miles from where we lived. I used to come home at dinner time. My brothers were so lucky to have bicycles, as I saw it looking back on that time. They used to give me a lift on the back, otherwise I had to walk. It sure was different in those days; no cars to worry about when it came to crossing the roads, on your own, as I recall.

During the Winter of 1950, when I was six years old, I can clearly remember the smog; it persisted all day. We had difficulty in seeing one another in the playground. Also that year, my Father bought a nine inch television which cost £100. I can remember the Korean War being on the news. One of the BBC Children's Hour programmes I used to like watching was Rolf Harris with his puppets. He used to sing 'Yi yi yippy yippy yi yi yiyiyi singing yi yi yippy yippy iy'. Other favorites of mine at that time were Norman Wisdom and Laurel and Hardy. I also remember Silver Peters, the announcer, telling us all about the next programme. I thought the BBC was wonderful and still do.

I used to love watching the beautifully-coloured butterflies flying about the Buddleia trees, and the lovely smell from the Buddleia tree flower. It's no wonder so many butterflies were attracted to this flower at the bottom of our garden - it seemed like hundreds when I was a child, which no doubt there was, but sadly today you might see one or two if you're lucky. I can see now, without knowing then, how much love I had for wildlife and animals. My Father used to keep pigs, goats and chickens. The pigs were reared for us; he bought a big double-door fridge to keep the pork in. Looking back, he sure was ahead of his time. It was 1969 when we bought our first chest freezer, which cost £100. I can remember one day, standing at our gate, watching the milkman coming down our road with his horse and milk float, and I so wanted to ask the milkman if I could stroke the horse. All of a sudden, the horse reared up and came running down the road at speed with the bottles and churns of milk all falling off the milk float. I watched in amazement.

Going out and about, the nearest town was Stains, and when I went there with my Mother, she used to put me on the back of her bicycle chair. If we went to Slough, we went by bus. Sometimes we would go to West Norwood in London. As we didn't live too far from London, we were able to travel up by train, which I loved to do as a child, to see Grandmother. In those days Windsor had two train stations; one was for the Great Western Region trains which were still steam-hauled in those days. The noise from the steam engine, especially when the valve blasted off, frightened me no end, without knowing what caused the noise. I could have never imagined that many, many years later, I would be working with these wonderful big steam engines, and what great engines they are too. The Great Western Station closed some years later.

Living where we did, we weren't far from London Airport as it was known then (it changed to Heathrow in 1965). The big four-engined propeller planes used to fly over our place. The biggest aircraft I saw was the Brabazon - I believe the biggest in the world flying at that time (it was scrapped in 1951). By this time my sister Christine was nearly three years old, so I had someone to play with apart from the children who lived up the lane from me. On my way home from school, I used to love to call on a farm and look in the pens where they used to keep the calves. I loved seeing the farm animals whenever I could, and I didn't imagine at that time, that I would be working with and looking after them when I was older. We also kept a nanny goat at home, which my Father used to milk. I was very fond of her.

1951-2

In 1951 my father had a fruit and vegetable business and drove a blue vehicle for his deliveries. Sadly, my Mother and Father separated that same year and my father sold the business. Life became a lot harder for us after Father's departure, despite him giving Mother the house. Mother met someone from Hampshire that same year and remarried, and that's when real problems began for us children. Especially for me. The bungalow was sold and before we knew it, on 12 December 1951, we found ourselves at Ibsley Drove, near Ringwood in Hampshire. Sadly, the goat I loved could not come with us as foot and mouth disease was rife at that time. The place Mother bought became a small holding eventually, but that was a little way off. It was the start of an unhappy period in our lives.

Ibsley Drove Bungalow

In January 1952 we started all over again at new schools. The first school I joined was Harbridge, about two miles from home. Being a very emotional child, I seemed to be in tears most of the time while I was there. As I got older, I realised I am one of those people who have a deep love for places I have lived, or even just stayed at, at home or in foreign lands. At that time, we had just moved and I was surely missing what was my home and land at Kedge Anchor in Fryer Road, Wraysbury, and of course our nanny goat whom I loved and still thought of. My brother and I had walked with her in the early evening and dark nights of December by moonlight. When she brayed, I used to give her a little cuddle... no one else in the family was affected but me.

The school in Harbridge closed in the early 60s so I went to the school at Rockford, about two miles from home and not far from Ibsley Aerodrome. I settled down after a while and made friends with other children of my age. At home there was all kinds of unimaginable trouble with our so-called stepfather. Although I do remember, as a child of 7 as I was then, that he gave me a single-decker London bus toy, which I treasured and still have to this day. I guess he must have liked me after all. He only stayed with us a few months however, as he wasn't prepared to work for us as a family, which meant there was little or no money coming into the household. These were tough times for us. After he went out of our lives, things settled down for a short time but more trouble started when Mother could not buy the land from the person who she bought the bungalow from - 7 acres was attached on the agreement, as I understood, that she had committed to buying. For the next eight years, the landowner gave us a lot of trouble.

In 1952 we had our first cow called Darky. Mother bought the cow from next door for £25, before the trouble started, and used to turn her out in the lane for her feed. Sometimes, my sister and I used to take Darky on a rope and lead her to where there were grass banks, but there was not really enough for her to eat. We did get about eight pints of milk a day and Mother made us lots of Ovalteen to drink which we liked. For me, milk was a life-saver as I didn't get a lot to eat at times, and they were tough times. Food rationing didn't help either.

I learned how to make junket, which only needed a teaspoonful of Rennet and sugar added to warm milk. I also had lots of cream, which came from our Jersey and Guernsey cows, when I learned how to milk them.

Me with Cow

The other thing that we missed as children was not having our television. It didn't become available to us again until 1954 when the transmitter on the Isle of Wight was built and we could receive a clear picture again. Back in 1952, things settled down after Mother was able to receive National Assistance of £4 per week to help us along. At the time we had one cow, a few chickens and one pig. My elder brother Brian had left school the previous year when we were still living at

Wraysbury. As I recall, after we moved, he then worked on a nearby farm looking after pigs. I learned later he didn't like farming at all. Neither of my two brothers had the same love for animals as I did.

Sometimes my brother Brian worked over at Hucklesbrook Farm making hay. Not too many years later, I worked on the same farm in the dairy, milking their cows. I loved being there and liked the family very much. In those days a lot of farms didn't have a baler to bale up the hay after it had been cut. It was common to put the hay into 'ricks' (hay piles). My other brother Geoffrey made a lot of friends from the 'sites', where there were 'Nissen huts' built for American troops during the Second World War. These became disused after the War and helped house many homeless people, as there was a great shortage of houses for people to live in at that time. We got to know most of the people that lived in them, having built up rounds for our peelings and vegetable collections.

1953

The King died in May of that year leading us into 1953, with the Coronation taking place on 2nd June 1953. We celebrated with a big bonfire on the common. My brother Geoffrey was one of the few chosen to carry the flaming torch to light the bonfire - they had a job to get it started as it had been so wet. That Spring we had a lodger who came to live with us. His father tried to make him come back home, but he was 21, and at 21 as I understood it, you could leave home, and that's what Walter intended to do, regardless of his father's wishes; he would live where he wanted to and not where his parents told him to. He had lived on Number Two site up until then, but that had blown over. He settled down to his new surroundings for the next five years or so.

Walter was very good to me that Summer. He bought me a new bike which cost £9. We went to Fordingbridge by bus where there was a nice bicycle shop. I came out of the shop feeling so proud holding my new bike. Walter walked me back holding the bike upright so I could partly ride it. The four-mile walk using the back roads to Ibsley Drove was wonderful, being a Summers evening. It took me a few weeks before I could just get on the bike and ride it. I used to climb on to the bike from the grass bank we had outside our place and ride it up the lane to the next high bank. It was very exciting having my own bicycle and being able to ride it without needing anyone to hold the bike.

With Walter's help, we started keeping more pigs, so we had to get more feed for them which was needed of course. Meal was about £1.10s per hundred weight. We went from house to house and to the sites asking people to save their peeling for us. Surprisingly enough most of them did, and we supplied them with bins to put the peelings in. We collected the peelings and boiled them to a high temperature in an old ion copper that was once used for boiling clothes in. There were plenty of old ion coppers around because more people must have started buying washing machines instead. Mother bought our first automatic washing machine in1961 which cost £100. Before the automatic came along, we had a big round machine with rollers to squeeze the water out of the clothes. I should know as Mother always seemed to get me to do that job - putting the clothes though the rollers. When the machine came, I was glad I didn't have that job to do any more.

With Mother's help, Walter bought an old 1936 truck to help collect the peelings, which turned out to be not very often! Sometimes we ended up pushing the vehicle back home, loaded with potatoes and vegetable peelings, which all had to be cooked up for the pigs. Despite a great deal of money being spent on it, many months later the truck ended up getting a frozen blockage (no anti-freeze!). So, it was back to the slog for me and my brother Geoffrey on our bikes. There were a lot of trade bikes around which we bought from Ringwood market for £3 or so. I guess more shops must have been replacing bikes with vans and that's why they were a little easier to come by. We kept our bicycles right through the 1950s. Coles of Stuckton, near Fordingbridge (still there to this day), transported all our animals to and from Ringwood Market, and sometimes Salisbury Market, and anything else we needed moving, such as furniture, at times. This continued until 1964, our last year at Forest View in Ibsley Drove.

Transport costs in those days were about £1 to £3, depending on the number of pigs that had to be taken, and it helped to keep the cost down when other people's goods were transported as well. The Coles family were very good to us during that time. Piglets used to fetch between £1 to £1.10s each, depending on size. When they were fattened up ready for pork, we were paid about £4 or £5 each, again depending on weight and the price paid per score (hundredweight) which varied from week to week, plus a Government subsidy.

Another job for us was getting bedding for the pigs, which meant going up onto the common to cut and bag bracken. We usually went on Sundays as a family so we could all help. It was hard work as only one or two bags could be carried on our bikes and it was a good mile there and back, passing what seemed to be big woods to me at the age of 9. The woods were so memorable because of the thousands of bluebells and daffodils, so wonderful to see, and brown squalls with their long brush-like tails, jumping from one tree to another – such great fun to watch them.

On the left side going up the hill was Wyatt's Farm. I learned, some eight years later, when I helped out milking cows here, that the owner had 70 acres. Just the kind of place I imagined owning. Further up we passed Number Two site, which was set in the woods, and Number Three site, just off the bend of the hill. Getting the bags of bracken back down the long hill home was hard going and had to be done nearly every week or so, depending on the amount we brought back. Straw cost about five shillings a bale. Mother always found it difficult to find the cash to buy hay or straw which we needed at times. I never understood why she didn't put any money by from the sale of the pigs or calves that I had reared. Anyone reading this story might say what a hopeless situation it all looked to be! My loyalty was fully stretched at times, what with the hay and straw, unless she had to do it, it seemed to me.

That same year, 1953, almost all the trees were cut down in the big wood next to Moyles Court. We bought off-cuts from this, delivered to us by Coles of Stuckton. We used to cut them into small pieces, with a two-handled saw, and burned them on our indoor Rayburn fire and for boiling the pigs' food outside.

By then our Alsatian puppy was just about a year old. We called her Greta and she was one of many to come in later years. This one had travelled from Cumberland, as it was known then, and it took a night and a day before she arrived at Ringwood Railway Station for collection by my Mother. Greta became a very good guard dog, even helping to round up pigs when they got out of their pigsties, which was quite often, as well as the calves. One of the things she was very good at was if she was told to sit and stay in an awkward place, where the calves or pigs could easily get through. She would stop them, enabling us to get in front and drive them back to where we wanted them to go. It was great fun as children having all these animals, apart from the work-side and feeding of them all.

As time went on, I began to really love the place as did my sister. Later, as children, we felt very free to do a lot of things that other children could not do, particularly where the animals were concerned, even though it was common for people to keep a pig or two in those days to help them along, and most places in the country had bigger gardens than we have today.

1953 was the first time in two years that my Mother was able to raise the train fare to take my older brother with her to go and see her Mother in West Norwood. The train fare would have been somewhere around £1.10s, and half fare for children as it is today. It was some three years before my sister and I could travel regularly up to London to see our grandmother, which we loved to do. My grandmother was born in Spain and met my grandfather when he was working in Gibraltar where he was in the Police Force. They came back to this country before the first World War and lived in London for the rest of their lives, where they went on to have eight children, three of which died later in life; two were lost in the war and my Mother's sister Betty died of a growth in her 20s. Mother's oldest brother went into the Police Force and worked his way up through the ranks. He ended up being Commander of Police until the late 1950s when he retired from the Force. As children we did not see so much of our Uncles after we moved from Wraysbury to Ibsley, near Ringwood. In those days, the time it took us to reach West Norwood, London, where our Grandmother and Grandfather lived, made it seem as if it was hundreds of miles away.

I remember my grandfather in his wheelchair as he had had his left leg amputated due to an infection. Sadly, our Grandfather passed away shortly after coming out of Hospital in 1952. That was the last time I saw him.

We caught the Wilts and Dorset bus, as it was known then, from the top of the Ibsley Drove early in the morning. (Wilts and Dorset buses changed to Hants and Dorset and has since changed back to Wilts and Dorset!). WH Smiths and Sons paper stall could be found at all railway stations – at Ringwood Station I looked at some comics while waiting for the 'Push and Pull' train from Bournemouth West. After waiting, you always knew when a train was coming as you could see the crossing gates being opened in the distance. Eventually, the train arrived then travelled on to Brockenhurst where it terminated. There was a long wait before the train came from Bournemouth to take us on to London. It must have taken three hours to get there. It was the last time we ever travelled from Ringwood to London. For our future visits, and there were many of them to London, we caught the 6pm bus from Ringwood which arrived at Ibsley Drove at 6.10pm and arrived in Salisbury for 7pm. This gave us about 45 minutes to walk up to Salisbury Railway Station for the train which left at 7.45pm and arrived in London Waterloo at 9.45pm. All trains were hauled by steam engines on the Western Region up until 1962, when diesel engines took over and services sped up considerably. Some 11 years later I joined British Rail.

1954

In January 1954, I went with the school party to Ringwood Cinema to see the crowning of the Queen. I found it very interesting as it reminded me of London. I knew a lot of children had not visited London. That year was quite a year for me as I suffered a great deal from a lot of illnesses; I was going deaf and was off from school for almost a whole term. By the Summer, I was experiencing great difficulty in reading and writing, even with extra help. I never did read or write properly for a long time to come. I never did like school. I'll never understand how my Mother, who had been privately educated, did not self-educated me. Sadly, she never helped me with my English.

The nice thing that year was sweet rationing came to an end and for us children. It was heaven being able to buy sweets again with our old pennies that we used to earn. We were also able to use our television set around that same time. Also around about that time, the fuel tanks that were placed underground, were taken up and used for refueling the Spitfires. As children coming home from school, we used to pass by on the way home and were always intrigued by it all. News went around that there was a secret trapdoor inside the control tower and that used to frighten us, so we never went in, until years later when it became obvious that there was no trapdoor after all.

Ibsley Aerodrome

Spitfires Fly Over Ibsley Aerodrome

Most of the Aerodrome was taken up in 1959. A few lorry loads came to the Drove to fill-in a lot of potholes. To this day, most of it is under water, and most of it was excavated for gravel. There was a big chemical factory run by BDH which used an aircraft hangar opposite the Aerodrome and employed a lot of people. We used to have some of the chaps lodging with us temporally while they were working there. The place was closed in 1958. Some years later, the former BDH aircraft hangar was taken down, and now it is a field once again.

1954 was the year we lost our white head dog, Pluto. A wonderful doggy he was. We had brought him with us from Wraysbury and he loved catching rabbits, which in those days were so easy to catch. Once he kept chasing one big rabbit up our Drove until the rabbit gave up. It weighed 6lbs - we ate it, the rabbit not the dog! One day Mother asked Walter, who was lodging with us at the time, to drive her, my sister Christine, my brother Brian and I in the back of the small truck to Holmesley, near Brockenhurst, where our Mother and Father went camping in the 1930s. Mother wanted to see this place again and show us exactly where it was they had camped. As a child, I was intrigued by the forest and where my Mother and Father had stayed all those years ago. We collected fallen pieces of wood here for our fire. Pluto loved rabbiting, and wasn`t missed, until we were about to leave when there was no sign of him. After we got home, Mother could not think of our Pluto being lost and nor could I, so we went back to Holmesley again, to the same place. It was raining I recall, and after a while of calling him, he turned up so pleased to see us, and so were we to see him. Such wonderful memories I still have of our Pluto whom I loved.

But, sadly that same year, we did lose him forever. He used to like going out with our cow, Darky, who we would turn out on the roadside for feed. I guess he must have gone rabbiting, but on the last occasion he did not come back with the cow at night. A few weeks later, there was a picture of a white-headed terrier in the *Daily Mirror,* saying it had been found wandering about. It looked just like our Pluto. It was sad for us as children not knowing where he had gone. Anyway, Mother wrote to the *Daily Mirror* without any luck. We also lost our cat that year. Why Mother let our Pluto go with the cow, we will never know. I shall never forget our Pluto whom I loved very much to this day.

Also, that same year, various didicoys called by to try and persuade Mother to buy a big removal lorry. This was of no use to us at all really because my older brother could not drive properly, although he was 18 years old. Walter, our lodger, was the same and couldn't drive properly either. I suppose they must have given her the idea that the lorry could have been used for transporting the animals and other things to market. Anyway, they must have persuaded her in the end. Only being 10 years old, I did not really know what was going on, only what Mother told me and what I remember. Mother didn't buy it from them, but she did a part-exchange for two big pigs and a car we had and £25 in cash. Well we were stuck with a big removal lorry that no-one could drive properly, but being something new to us children, we got quite excited about going for a ride in it. One day, when Mother was out, my older brother took all of us for a ride in it up the Drove. He drove like a madman. The Drove being a rough road made it worse. We were thrown about in the back of the lorry, or even in the front - it made no difference, he just found it funny. On one occasion I was in the front with him when we were going around a corner up at the sites, when the passenger door flew open and by chance, I caught hold of the steering wheel, otherwise I would have been thrown out. After that we didn't think it was fun anymore, so we didn't go in it again; but my sister and I did play in the back, pretending that the dogs were pigs or calves and getting them to go up the ramp. That seemed good fun to us.

Removal Lorry

1955-6

A few months later, Mother advertised the lorry in the Exchange and Mart. She didn't have much luck at first, but someone offered to part-exchange a caravan and some cash which turned out to be a good deal for us. It was another place for us to play in, and later it was let for something like £3 per week, which was a great help to us at that time. In 1955, our first tenant in the caravan was someone from Tonbridge in Kent, who answered our advertisement as she had separated from her husband. She had one son about my age, called Lesley. He became like a brother after only a few months. We had a lot of fun and he was liked by the other lads of my age at school, probably because of some of the things he was put up to by some of the lads - like knocking on people's doors and then running away when they answered the door, and anything else that could be thought of. He was very good at helping us about the place while he was staying with us. We had a lot of fun together, along with my sister. We had these steel wires called air-raid shelter wires. We bent them over, covering the wire with blankets, and climbed on top of our air-raid shelter and made our camp inside. It was nice and sunny round by the side of the bungalow where the shelter was, and a good hiding place too.

Lesley's mother worked at a nursery that Summer of 1955, mainly picking daffodils and tulip heads off so as to increase the bulbs the following year. She was a good friend to my Mother while she was staying with us in the caravan she rented. We used to cycle over to Harbridge and pick up all the dried grass from the verges and banks by the side of the road that had been cut by the Council. We would bring it back in bags and dry it out by spreading it about, then made a small rick of it. Once it was dry, it was a great help in the Winter for feeding our cows. A lot of us brought bags of hay back. On the 1st August 1956, Bank Holiday as it was in those days, we all went to Fordingbridge Cinema with Lesley and his mother for the last time. We said goodbye as we walked up the cinema aisle, on our way out. Sadly, we never did see or hear from Lesley or his mother again. For me it was a very emotional time for some time after, because it felt as if I had lost a brother as we were similar in age. "Life had to go," as Mother used to say.

During the Winter of 1955 I went to the Ringwood Senior School with the other lads to see if I was going to be any good at the 11+ exam. I soon found out, when I did move up in September that year, that I hadn't passed any of those exams. At the time there seemed to be a lot like me who didn't pass many exams - about 40 of us boys and girls. The class they put us in was called 'Remove'; why it was given that name, nobody ever knew. I guess someone must have thought we had no hope, however hard we tried. Apart from the gardening lessons, which I regarded myself as being good at, and I liked gardening very much and got the highest marks for, I hated school. A lot of the teachers were just bullies, with no interest in who would have been described as 'backward' children. My sister and other children at that time thought the same about school.

The 'Remove' children were placed in an old Cadets' hut. We had to cross Hightown Road, opposite the school, and go down some steps. The hut was at WH Wards and Sons, the scrap merchants which has since closed down, and the old hut has been pulled down too. I remained there with the other kids until September 1957, when were moved into the main school building, and I was here until I left in 1959. The new school started being built in 1957 which I attended for one term in 1959. In all the time I was there, I did try to do better and get myself out, but never came anywhere near the mark that was required of me. Losing a lot of days off for health reasons also didn't help. By then we had a lot more animals to look after.

HAMPSHIRE EDUC[illegible]N COMMITTEE
SCHOOL REPORT

Ellingham C.E. SCHOOL

NAME Christopher Brettell Class or Standard Upper Juniors

Age 11 years 5 months Position in Class

Average Age of Class 10 years Number in Class

SUBJECT	Max. Marks	Marks Gained	Teacher's Remarks
Mathematics			Christopher was not here to take the examination.
English: Reading			
Composition			He is still backward for his age, but he works & tries very hard.
Recitation			
Writing			
Geography			He is very good indeed with all practical work; kind & obliging & very trustworthy in every way.
History			
Drawing			
Needlework			
Nature Study			
Physical Training			
Music			He has good manners & a nice way of speaking.
TOTAL			

Number of openings Attendance Fair. Times absent Times late

Conduct V. Good

Head Teacher's Remarks: Christopher is most interested in all branches of farming & is good at gardening.

Date 22 July 1955 [illegible] Head Teacher

Parents are asked to tear off and return this slip to the Head Teacher

I acknowledge the receipt of my son's / daughter's School Report

Date (Signed) Parent

School Report

In Easter 1955, my brother Geoffrey left school and started work on a farm at Linford, but didn't stay more than a year. I was led to believe from what Mother told me at the time that he didn't like working on his own. My brother Geoffrey wouldn't have told me if I had asked him. As for me, I had become more and more interested in gardening. I used to dig up certain sections of our one and a quarter acres, and instead of using fencing to keep the animals out, I would dig up the old turf grass and turn it over so as to rot the grass down and make a wall around the area I had dug up. Then I planted it out with peas, beans and potatoes, with Mother's help. After a week or two, my sister and I would dig up some of the seeds just to see if the seeds had taken. I couldn't wait for them to come up.

Before leaving Rockford School that year, I used to help out in the Headmistress' garden after school and earn a couple of shillings each time. That same year I was able to ride my bike on the main road, so it enabled me to cycle to Fordingbridge Fish Shop to pick up all the fish and any other waste that they put in the collection containers. Geoffrey used to ride a three-wheeler bike which was once used for transporting ice-cream on the seafront. It had two wheels on the front of the bike and one on the back. It took quite a lot of hard pedalling to push the bike along, loaded with smelly fish in hot weather. Luckily for us, on those hot sunny days we hardly met any cars or lorries on the A388 Salisbury Road; it used to take us two or three hours to ride there and back to Ibsley Drove, after which we would boil the fish up for the pigs. Sometimes in the hot weather there were thousands of maggots in the bins and they were boiled up as well.

It was easy going in our Summer holidays and other holidays, but not so good in other parts of the year. To keep the contract with the Fish Shop, we needed to pick up once or twice a week, depending on how busy they were and the time of year. It was that much harder going in the Winter for us, so, as we were having difficulty in picking up regularly, one of the sons kindly brought the fish out to us in a van for a while. But this didn't last long; they stopped bringing the fish out to us for no reason, but I guess, looking back, Mother never offered anything towards the cost of petrol (about 3 shillings a gallon). In 1956, when that ended, it left us with a gap without any feed for the pigs. We bought Barley meal for a while and started new rounds in Ringwood and Fordingbridge, collecting swill. We had to do this to keep the feeding costs down.

That same year, my older brother Brian was called up for National Service. By then, Geoffrey, my sister Christine and I were doing a lot more work about the place. Walter, our lodger, also made a big contribution to the household at the time. My older brother Brian didn't like farm work I remember rightly. When he wasn't working, he would be listening to the *BBC Light Programme* as it was known then; from *Housewives' Choice* to *Mrs Dale's Diary* and anything else that was worth listening to, rather than work.

Before Brian went into the Army, Mother got a job at the roadside hotel known as the 'As You Like It' near North Gorley on the A388 Salisbury Road between Ibsley and Fordingbridge. A lot of the people use to stay there in the four chalets that have since been turned into bungalows and sold off. It was a good time for me that Summer. I went to the hotel a few times while Mother was working. I used to cut down all the stinging nettles taller than me. I liked doing this kind of work even though I was only 11 years old. The grass bank near the hotel was hard to do. I was given a good dinner and a few shillings for helping out. Our lodger Walter managed to get a job with a building firm called Brazier, as there was a lot of building going on in Bournemouth at the time, around the Landsdown. It was easy to remember because whenever we went to Bournemouth on the bus, Walter would point out the places he was working on as they were on the bus route. For most of the time that Walter worked down there, he had to cycle the 12 miles each way; sometimes, he used to get a lift with someone he knew from Ringwood.

Later that year, Brian was finally called up after being delayed by a few months, and Mother was upset for days. None of us had ever been away from home before, so that made it worse. Later on, Mother tried to get him out of the Army, but that came later… Brian had to travel to Oswestry in North Wales for six weeks of training. He was then transferred to West Moors Army Camp for the next two years. From what I saw of his two years in the Amy, it seemed to be a bit of a waste of time to me.

Our first cow Darky finally dried up that year, so she had to be sent to market. We were without a cow for a little while and that meant being without milk of our own. Having our own cow had provided a good six or seven pints per day. Milk cost about 3d (pence) a pint to buy then. There were occasions when the cow didn't come back at night for milking or didn't turn up at all. We very often informed the New Forest Agister, the man who would look for missing animals, who usually found her as he knew the area very well. On one occasion, Darky went missing for over a week and when she was found by the New Agister, she was eight miles the other side of Linwood in the New Forest, so she had to be driven back 13 miles, invariably single-handed. It was no easy task getting her away from the herd that she had tagged on to, and they had wandered further miles searching for food. My eldest brother and Walter had to tramp in the snow just to make matters worse. This is what contributed to the cow drying up that much quicker, which they are apt to do if not milked regularly.

Luckily for us, the cow disappearing like that never did happen again in all the years that followed. We didn't get very much for the cows when we sold them; one never does for Jersey cows as their meat is a yellow meat and isn't worth as much as Friesian cows. After selling Darky, a few weeks later we bought another Jersey cow, but sadly we were only able to keep her for a year. We named her Daisy. At the time, the Ministry of Agriculture introduced a testing system whereby a vaccine was injected into the cows' necks, and if a bump came up after a week, then there was a good chance that the cow would have TB. In our case, Daisy had TB. All cattle found to have the disease were slaughtered, so that was the end of her sadly for me. I had grown to love all these animals.

We even got less for her than we hoped, so were unable to buy another cow at that time. Luckily for us, a lot of small holding farmers that Mother knew clubbed together and bought us a Guernsey cow and we named her Buttercup. She was a very friendly cow. By the following year, 1957, Buttercup had also developed TB so that was the end of her. It seemed worse this time as she was given to us. Somehow, we got over it. We were without a cow for a couple of months but then bought another Jersey cow from a friend of Mother's out at Matchams, near Ringwood. This one was named Hopey, a very good milker, and she was small but could kick like a donkey. When I was able to milk her by hand, my hands, wrists and arms used to ache like hell, and being afraid of the animal, I would just put down the stall and bucket ready to start milking her and she would start kicking me and that made me even more afraid of her. I stuck at it. I'd quieten her down, get about two or three pints in the bucket and then she would give an almighty kick and the bucket would go flying, and I would end upon on the floor. I was so mad with her. Mother would hear all this going on, come in and shout at her, but it didn't really do a lot of good, and it wasn't much help for me only being 13. I wasn't all that strong. I kept on with it every day, and in the end, I was no longer afraid of her and she turned out to be a nice friendly cow.

A few months later, we bought another Guernsey cow from the same place over at Matchams. Her name was Alex. She was a very big cow for a Guernsey, and in many ways a lot like a bull. If she wanted to get into the shed where we kept the cattle cake, she would push the door in and eat as much as she could reach. The Co-op Baker would leave bread for us in the bread bin with a lid on it. Sometimes if no-one was there after the baker had gone and the cows were there, they would knock the lid off and eat the four loaves of bread. Alex would come indoors if the door was open to get at the bread.

Those early years in 1956 and 1957 saw a major change in the way cows looked as they were dehorned, which meant the horns that grow out of their heads were cut off. They were injected first so they didn't feel any pain, and then the vet would use an ordinary saw to cut as close as possible to the head so as to avoid any lumps sticking out. In my view, once the cows' hair had grown over the horn, they looked nicer. Surprisingly, a lot of older farmers didn't like the idea at first, but soon realised that they could keep a lot of cattle in a more confined space as it stopped fighting amongst the animals, particularly at feed time. The next generation of farmers and young calves saw the cows being dehorned at the early age of a few weeks old. Again, they would be injected in the head and a hot iron was fitted over the stub of the horn to burn it out until you got to the core of the horn, otherwise it would grow again. Originally, you would have to wait until you had a fully-grown cow before being able to dehorn it.

Being unaware of cows bringing their heads up quickly (when tying them up, you tended to put your head over theirs') my Mother once leant too far over the cow's head and was butted by the horn which knocked her silly. It happened to me some years later, not through lack of experience, but by being over-confident with the cow not having horns. When tying them up for milking I was hit in the teeth and had a cracked tooth, but luckily not anything too serious. On the lighter side of cows having horns, my brother Geoffrey and I used to like to wrestle with our Jersey cows as they weren't particularly strong. We were able to grab hold of their horns and tried to tip them over. We must have thought we were the American cowboys, being young and rough and ready for anything. When the calves were strong enough to support us on their backs, we would ride them. We never stayed on for long - we usually fell off, but it was good fun.

Once I was able to milk a cow, another trick I liked playing on other children, was to say, "Have you ever seen milk come out of a cow?", and the usual answer would be "No". "Then I will show you," I would say. The kiddies would be very enthusiastic about where the milk came from, and for me good fun. I would go up to our cow Hopey, and, being the lovely, friendly Jersey cow she was, I would stroke her to stop her moving away. Then I would get a nice lot of milk in her teat and get the kids to look down at it and I would squeeze as hard as I could. Bearing in mind that I was only 13 years old and not very strong in the hand, as I hadn't been milking Hopey very long. But she would let her milk down for me which I sprayed straight in their faces! We all found it very funny with milk on their faces. I think Hopey did too.

The summer of 1956 was my first working Summer holiday - harvesting, something I had never done before. It involved following the binder and tractor around the field after it had cut the corn into bundles. There were usually six to eight of us taking a row each, putting the bundles into aisles so as to keep the corn dry in wet weather, which was quite frequent. If it rained for too long, all the aisles would have to be pulled apart and the bundles opened so they could dry out. The reason for all this extra work was because grass seed was sown at the same time as the corn, therefore it took a lot longer to dry out both before they could be put into 'ricks'. There would be about four people on the rick, building it, and one on the trailer or horse and cart. At that time, the farm only had one tractor and two shire horses, with which I did a lot of work the following year. The work was slow going if the weather was against us or we were short-handed. Most of the extra labour was done by part-timers, and a lot of young lads like me getting a shilling an hour.

Most of the Summer, during harvesting time, would have meant working Saturdays and Sundays to gather the corn in during good weather. With a lot of help, the hundred acres or so of wheat and barley were put into ricks to store to be thrashed-out during the Wintertime. Some of the corn and barley was grown in what became fields around Ibsley Aerodrome, which was used during the Second World War. Some of the older chaps who helped out during harvest time had been in the War, in some cases both Wars, and we were all interested in what they told us about their involvement. We loved working in that area. Harvesting usually finished before the end of August, subject to good weather conditions. I don't know what the other lads spent their hard-earned money on, but I did like to give Mother a box of Black Magic, which cost 5 shillings, and weighed 1lbs. I also contributed to the household, which Mother expected, and bought some sweets for myself, something we had very little of as children. I tried to save some money and sometimes bought two and sixpenny saving stamps.

The new term in September 1956, my second year at Ringwood Senior School, meant a lot of pals who were a year younger than me moved up to being in their first year. One in particular, Terry, turned out to be a very good friend, and his family were great too. He shared the same interest in farming which we both loved. He started off in the same class as me, and a couple of years later moved up to a higher class. My other good friend was Tony Fitzgerald, who years later got his own small garage business servicing cars. He has been looking after my cars and trucks bought over the years ever since I started my landscape garden business in July 1980, when I had left British Rail after 13 years of service.

It made school life a little better for me having someone I had known a long time. I changed buses to go in with Terry. I had been catching the 8.20am number 38 bus (still running today) which only took ten minutes to get to Ringwood, but meant waiting half an hour before school started which I hated, so I used to walk about the town before going in. When I changed buses to the one which I knew Terry and other lads travelled on, I was a lot happier and we didn't arrive until 8.50am, or a little later. If that bus ran late getting to Ringwood, it made it hard for me as I had to deliver two pints of milk every weekday morning before starting school. I would get off the bus and run down the hill, around the corner past the Railway Station and leave the two pints of milk and pick up the empty bottles from the day before. But first I had the day in front of me so I would have to run all the way back up the hill towards school, nine times out of ten just making it for 9am. Mother could pick up six shillings per week for this milk run. Looking back, I find it hard to think that I didn't get even one shilling a week for all this running about - bigger fool me. That's loyalty for you. It was the same going home.

So as to get home in good time, to be with my animals waiting for me to feed them, I would run down the bit of hill, round a sharp bend to the bus stop, to try and catch the 4 o'clock. School time ended at 3.55pm which gave me a better chance to catch the bus. I had to cross the main road first, which was near the Railway crossing, but if the bus ran a minute or so early, and if I saw that I had missed the bus by a minute, I would run down to the Market Square opposite the Church where it departed from at 4pm, and try to catch the bus from here. The buses had no doors to contend with so you could just jump on. When that happened, which was quite often, it meant running a mile from the Station. Nine times out of ten I caught it and was home by 4.15pm. Later, the times were changed at the school, so everybody came out at 3.50pm. This made it even easier for me to catch the bus from the Station. Eventually, I travelled on the original school bus I used to take in the mornings, which ran from the opposite end of the Drove and usually got home usually by 4.35pm.

About this time, with so many swill rounds to do, after arriving home from school I used to ride back to Northfield Road in Ringwood to collect peelings for the pigs. It used to take me a good hour or so. On these occasions my brother Geoffrey would milk the cows and feed the pigs too. Thank heavens for that, I would say to myself. Otherwise every day was much the same: hard work.

In December 1956 we had the fire grate taken out which had been in the bungalow since it was built in 1939. This was because we were able to afford to buy and install a new Rayburn. We were glad the grate was taken out as we couldn't cook anything on it and it very often used to smoke us out of the room. So when the Rayburn was put in its place with a new hot water tank, it made a big difference in heating our very cold bungalow, as well as being able to cook on it as we didn't have an electric cooker either as we relied on oil stoves. Even when we did eventually have an electric cooker, Mother didn't like using it as she always said it used too much electricity. The hot water tank was next to the Rayburn in an airing cupboard. There was a lot of room underneath the tank and it was very warm so we came up with the idea of keeping chicks here, which we did, usually 50 at a time. We did this for about four years. I must have reared hundreds of chicks during that time. They were kept indoors only in the Winter. We put an electric light in the cupboard to keep the chicks warm when the tank was cool, which helped keep them quiet as well. I used to clean them out regularly.

In the Spring of 1955, my Mother had tried to meet with our Member of Parliament, Crosswaight Aires, about getting my older brother Brian out of the Army. She saw the MP's agent in Ringwood, and I went with her. When the agent was taking details, he asked how many animals we had. Mother's answer was she didn't know exactly. When I was older, looking back on it, I do not recall Mother ever receiving a reply - if she had, I am sure she would have told me. Most likely after they had looked at Mother's request, they didn't regard our farm as big or important enough for my brother Brian to come out of the army a year or so before completing his National Service.

Later that year, my other brother Geoffrey left the farm at Linford as he didn't like working on his own. With all the TB testing going on during that time, there was a temporary milking job going at Hucklesbrook Farm, but this wasn't at the main Diary at the farm, it was in a temporary brick-built cow pen at one of the disused RAF Nissen huts. The few cows that had failed the TB testing were kept separately here. This was to keep the milk separate as well and lasted for a few weeks until the animals who failed the retest were phased out. My brother continued to work at the farm right up until April 1959 when the TB testing came to an end. Geoffrey then went to work at Bickham's Bakery House which was by the railway level crossing gates; he found it hard going working inside and having to work at night baking bread. 1959 was also a very hot summer. Geoffrey bought himself a good motorbike with his wages.

1957

1957 saw the beginning of the new Secondary Modern school getting well underway. It was a quiet year for me, apart from having our new cows, Hopey and Alex, and we started to have a few calves. Alex was a very good mother to other calves, and she reared many over the years we had her. One calf in particular, I named Honeybell, I looked after all the way through her life. She was a pretty Jersey calf that I reared to a milking cow.

Me with Calf

Hopey

In October 1957, I saw a Jet flying low overhead and it crashed a minute or so later in a ball of fire over the common, just missing a house called Cuckoo Hill where I was to work in the garden for two years, some five years later. As it wasn't far from where we lived, I cycled up in the semi-darkness. It was a moonlit night, as I recall, and a lot of the local people did the same. When we got there, the aircraft was still burning but luckily the pilot had ejected and as far as we know he survived.

Spitfire over Three Tree Hill

Towards the end of 1957, Walter our lodger was becoming unsettled. He got friendly with a family that he knew when he lived on Number Two Site. Why? We do not know, other than wanting a change perhaps. But as time went on he had become unreliable, which was sad as he had been such a great help to us overall and seemed quite happy during the time he stayed with us. We heard later that he intended to live with the family as a farmhand in the tied cottage, which we didn't know anything about until the day it happened. They finally moved in May 1958, to Warminster we learned. But to our surprise, he came back to us the same day that the family moved out from Number Two Site, and he told us all kinds of reasons why he didn't go with them. A short time after, he just upped and went, where to Heaven knows? We never saw or heard from him from that day to this. I was sad about that too.

1957 saw my older brother Brian come out of the Army. He didn't have a job to start with, but after a being at home for a while, he got a job at Ringwood Regal Cinema, as a film projectionist, but that didn't last very long. He went to see about a job at British Railways, as it was known then, and started work as Porter at West Moors Station; one week earlies, 6am-2pm, and one week lates, 2pm-10pm. He had to cycle from Ibsley to West Moors via Horton Road. Once he settled into the job and got to know the chaps quite well, he was able to catch the paper train, which ran via Ringwood Station, instead of cycling all the way to West Moors. It made life a little easier for a 6am start. After two years of late and early turns, and doing station portering at West Moors, he then became a travelling 'Shunter' which included work at West Moors, Wimborne and Ashley Heath Railway Goods Yards. It's a wonder that the station platform is still there for all to see today, as all the station buildings and the line were since destroyed. He wanted a change, so he transferred to Ringwood Station as a lorry driver. That was in 1960, but first, he had to learn how to drive a lorry. He did have some idea of how to drive a lorry from the one we had for a while. I said to him for a laugh he probably passed his real test in the Goods Yard. Being a rough road, you could hear his lorry coming almost from the top of the Drove when the wind was in the right direction. You would know it was our Brian.

After knocking down a gate post and churning up the road, making it very muddy outside our gate, he blocked the entrance with his lorry. It became another way of life. He should have left his lorry at the station yard, but as he used to deliver cattle cake and other feed stuff for pigs and chickens to all the farms in the area, it wasn't very often he would get back to the Goods Yard before it was closed for the night. All the animals' feed stuff used to be made at Avonmouth, near Bristol, and was transported in trucks on British Railways. Small loads were shunted off at Goods Yards for unloading and delivery to the farms in the area. When most of the Goods Yards closed in the late 1960s and 70s, all animal feed stuff was transported by road straight from where it was made to the farms. Silcox were the main suppliers at that time for this area.

1958

After the Suez Crises and the petrol rationing of 1956 was over, I saw a general increase in the number of vehicles on the road. By the Spring and Summer of 1958, having extra cows meant we were able to rent ground - a great relief for me and the cows well. My heart was in farming and I lived in the hope that we would have our own ground to keep the cows on and off the main roads. As a youngster, it was tough going as the cows liked to travel further afield and they always seemed to find their way up onto the main road. Even so, we drove them towards the back roads so as to keep them off the main road, because there were so many cars on the road. One of their favourite spots was over at Harbridge, which meant driving them back a good mile or so. But first they had to be found and that mean cycling to their favourite places, and if there was no sight of them, cycle on to the next place; that could have been from Ibsley, or Ibsley Church, or Ellingham or back the other way towards Hucklebrook, or even further on, only a mile or so from Fordingbridge. It was very difficult on one's own and especially when it had been a hot day. The flies would aggravate the cows and they could be very awkward, trying to go back the way they just came or crossing the road in front of cars, and with me getting dreadful looks from drivers. Only being 13 years old made it that much harder for me to cope with at times. Once I had got them going, after some hairy moments, it would have taken anything from half an hour to an hour to get them back home.

Before we rented ground, we only had an acre of ground all told, which didn't give us very much grass to feed the cows on all the time. We mainly kept them in at night, but sometimes they were turned out in the evening and that meant getting up early in the morning to look for them. To make it easier to find them, we put a bell around one of the cow's necks. But letting them out at night must have annoyed someone no doubt, because we found the cows all right, but no bell which must have been taken off her; it was a help while it lasted. In all the 12 years, from 1952–1964, when they finally put grids in at the entrances of each forest road leading to the main road, none of our cows were knocked down, but we did have a few near misses on the main road when driving them in the semi-dark on the very odd occasion. There was a funny side when driving the cows along the main road in the Summertime. Usually I would be getting the cows back by about teatime, and that meant there would be some people having a picnic just at the entrance of our Drove. Some people, being scared of cows, would move out of the way and the cows would eat whatever they could get hold of - the lettuce, bread or anything else they fancied, I guess. Very embarrassing for me!

This went on for a further five years but in between that time we did rent a piece of ground from the Post Office, which was known as a telephone exchange, just along the main road not far from the top of the Drove. It made life easier for us while it lasted, but we couldn't have it all the time. In those days the grass here looked like lawns with all the cattle and horses eating it right down low.

In 1958 I was really getting into farming, building up the stock at home with the amount of pigs we had – 30 to 40 by this time. We also had several hundred chickens and we used to send the eggs to the egg packing station in Ringwood, which was near the Railway Station (both have gone now). The eggs were collected every Wednesday and a cheque was sent every month, and we used to sell a lot of eggs locally as well. By this time we were breeding our own pigs. We had four sows by now; each of them had 9 to 12 piglets twice a year. Some of the pigs we reared for pork and the rest were sent to Ringwood Market and would sell for between £4-6, depending on how big they were.

By now we found the need to buy more straw instead of spending so much time going up to the common to get bracken for their bedding. In the Winter, the sows needed to be kept warmer with their piglets otherwise they would have died.

One sow I will always remember was a big, black saddleback. This sow we bought from the Coopers who were living up at the sites then, but had to move to Ringwood that year, so gave up keeping pigs. She was a very unfriendly sow, and when she had her piglets you had a job getting into the pigsty for cleaning out and littering up purposes. Once I went in there after she had her litter and I found myself being under attack and not being able to get out. I only had the fork to defend myself. When she moved away from the entrance of her sleeping place, I jumped over the wall and didn't go back in when she was in there. I think we used to let her out or drive her into another sty so that we could clear the sty out properly. This sow had a very long snout. We only kept her for a few months - no doubt she ended up as sausage meat, which all sows did.

By the Spring of that year I was working regularly on Saturday mornings over at the farm. One of the jobs that became regular was leading the shire Horse in between the rows of kale which would be the cows' Winter feed. I had to walk in between the kale rows with the lovely shire Horse, Violet. This is known as 'Horse Hoeing'. I must have walked miles and covered a lot of acreage, which was very tiring, for about 3 ½ hours at a time. But that was the last time that year the fields were hoed using the Horse with me leading her. It was replaced with a tractor hoeing implement which was attached to the back of the tractor, and one could sit on it to guide it in between the kale rows, a lot less tiring than having to walk up and down which I did for three years during the sowing season.

In the Spring of 1958, I was 14 years old and Easter holidays were spent over at the farm working with Violet the Shire Horse. She had a very good temperament and a lovely Shire Horse she was. I was sure glad that at 14 years old I had the opportunity to have worked with her. I was able to get her to walk-on while I jumped off the cart and ran on ahead to open the gate; she would trot on through the gateway and stop when called to do so while I closed the gate. Like most lads of my age in those days, I usually started off cleaning up the yard after or during milking time. Not being used to doing the job, I always ended up with cow dung all over me. It was a long time before I could keep myself clean which I did manage when I took on the full-time job when I became 15 years old. Having milking experience with our cows on our own small holding, enabled me to milk their Dairy of 80 or so Friesian cows they had at that time. Nowadays Dairies have herds of around 200 cows in large parlours which replaced cow pens.

Me on Horse

It was hard going harnessing the Shire Horse, and it was a struggle for me lifting the harness on to the horse's back. Taking it off again wasn't any easier. Once I had got her harnessed, I then lead her to the cart, backed her in, connecting the harness onto the arms of the cart. The cart was used specifically for transporting manure, after shovelling up all the cow dung and slop, all good for the ground, from where the cows stood in the yard earlier that morning, waiting to go into the cow pen to be milked. There was plenty of cow dung slop, especially in wet weather in Wintertime too. It all had to be shovelled on to the cart by hand and then transported up and shovelled onto the big manure heap. At the time I used the biggest shovel one could buy then. 50 years on, I have the same sized shovel and still use it to this day. Later on, the Shire Horse and manure cart was replaced by a tip-up trailer which was attached to a tractor. By the Summer of that year, both Shire Horses had sadly gone from the farm, retired from working on the land and replaced by tractors.

Saturday 8th August 1958 saw the launch of Southern Television. I did not want to go harvesting late into the evening, just wanted to watch the new and exciting programmes. By this time, I had had quite a bit of experience in rick building. There would be four or five of us building the ricks and usually three other lads would also be helping. Two of us would stand each side of the elevator, waiting for the sheaves to come. We would pass the sheaves to be put around the outside of the rick in order to get it square. Then we would fill in the middle and level up and start again with the next trailer load. It was a wonderful experience building these ricks and working with the lads I knew, all similar ages too. By the time we reached the very top of the rick, which would be very high, only two people would be left to finish off, and it would be left to the older chaps with a great deal of experience.

Hayrick Bygone Days

1958 was a wet Summer, so the harvesting continued well after we had gone back to school, and for me, it was the last Summer that I would have to think about going back to school after the holidays. Thank heaven for that, I said. With harvesting still going on well into late September that year, and with less daylight, it meant some of the harvest was lost due to the wet conditions. I used to help out on Saturdays. It was decided to place the sheaves which hadn't dried out in the woods, for the pheasants to eat the corn and barley. From the sheaves, the straw would eventually rot down, and was good for the birds to scratch about in. For us, with our cows, being a wet Summer meant that there was more grass on the roadside, and somehow there seemed to be less traffic on the main road, I expect due to it being a wet Summer.

By and large, Mr. Sampson of Hucklesbrook Farm was very helpful to me. As it was me paying for the hay and straw, I could get it cheaper from the farm, and it also saved us a lot of hard work in not having to go and get bracken from the common for the pigs' bedding, and not having to collect grass from the roadside. The following year also saw the end of collecting peelings for me – we only had about a half dozen places or so to collect from and I was able to delegate the job.

That same year, 1958, saw us with a second Alsatian dog with the aim of breeding. But this dog was a fully grown Alsatian and wasn't very friendly toward us, so Mother decided to hand him back to Ted Rodgers from whom she had bought him on a trial basis, as he was a family friend of ours. We did get a younger one, Carlo, who was about six months' old. He was a nice dog but with one drawback - he did like to stray sometimes - but apart from that, we had him five years and he fathered a lot of Alsatian puppies with Greta, our first Alsatian. In 1959 she had nine puppies. They all survived and sold for around 10 guineas each.

Once I had started full time work, earning £3 six shillings and 7d for a 48-hour week, I had a few spare shillings. I was able to pay my sister, Christine Rosemary, five shillings which was a lot for her and was to any of us when you didn't have any money, to cycle all the way to Ringwood to pick up the last few peelings. Mother insisted that the peelings were collected, as long as they were being saved for us, each week. One of the places my sister used to cycle to, was where I used to deliver the two pints of milk every school day until I left. My sister had little or no money ever come her way. It rarely crossed our mothers mind to give us any money to spend on ourselves or buy us sweets. The only money that came my way before earning, was when mother sent me shopping, and if there was any change, if I was lucky, I got 3d which I would spend on half penny chews. The milk delivery was continued by my brother each day, as he used to work with Mr. and Mrs. Rogers. That came to an end when they moved to Guernsey. All the Nissen huts were slowly going and most of the people we knew were being rehoused in and around Ringwood. That left hardly any peelings to collect locally, and I had had enough of cycling miles for a few old peelings. Slowly Mother was coming around to buying meal for the pigs instead.

1959-60

In 1959 with only about three months left at school to go, the new secondary modern had just been completed. All the new pupils went straight to the new school which had partly opened on the start of the new school term in September 1958. With the new school fully operational, both schools that I had started at in 1952 had closed. The start of the new term at the brand-new school in January 1959 saw us in nice new surroundings. But for me, with less than three months to go, and not enough time to really benefit from the new conditions and new techniques that were being offered in education here, it was too late.

At the beginning of 1959, our Alsatian dog Greta had eleven puppies. Losing two, she reared nine puppies altogether, and most of the puppies went to different parts of the country. It was expected of me to cycle all the way down to Ringwood on the trades bike with two tea chest boxes on the front with one puppy in each box. I arrived at Ringwood railway station only to find that the boxes were too small and they wouldn't accept them. So I took them back home, and cycled back down again the next day, this time with bigger boxes which were accepted, and they were sent off to the North of the country. I think Mother must have thought I had endless energy and at the same time, took advantage of my willingness to help at all times. She wouldn't have asked my older brother Brain, that's for sure.

The year I left school, in late March 1959, was one of the best days of my life. That same month I began working and was very excited about not having to go school anymore. I started work for Mr. Sampson at Hucklesbrook Farm, where I had worked the previous three years during my holidays. I only worked part-time at first, starting at 7.30am until 12.30pm lunch time. I found it hard going at first, with less time now in the mornings than I had when I was going to school, like most would at my age. Having to milk the cows and feed the calves and feed the pigs before seven, have my breakfast, then cycle over to the farm and start work there, right from the start, I never arrived on time, or anywhere else for that matter unless it suited me to as I always had jobs. Apart from the milk round job which I took on in 1964 with Unigate Dairies, that is. In those days it was a 5am start. And be there. It suited the employers to ask me to do some jobs that others couldn't do or didn't want to do, like milking the cows on Saturday afternoons and Sundays; the same applied to all the other jobs that followed.

I had been working part-time for a couple of months and only getting about £2.10s per week. Our Mother, being the kind of person she was, expected us to pay half of what we earned in keep at home and for buying clothes for working in. The Co-op had a clothes shop in Ringwood. My Mother was a member which meant you were paid a dividend for just about everything one bought. You were also able to join the £10 club, as it was called. For me it was a blessing, being local as well, as I had very little money to call my own. As soon as I was able to earn a few shillings in my school holidays, I bought a couple of pairs of jeans which I liked to wear very much.

Working some Saturday afternoons paid £1.10d per hour and £2.4d per hour for Sundays. I had some considerable experience in milking cows, but not with milking machines. However, as I knew the basics of milking cows, it didn't take long to learn how to use them, ie to know when the cow was milked, then take the milking machine cups off the cows' udders. Washing the cows' udders was also important too, which I was aware of many years ago, as cleanliness is obvious in my way of thinking.

All the time I lived in hope that we would be able to buy some land and set up in farming on our own. However small it might have been, it would have been better than turning the cows to eat the grass on the roadside, especially for me, as having to go looking for them after work made it hard going. Sometimes I would go straight from work and look for them, and more often than not, I couldn't find them, which meant having to go out again after tea, and very often look over the same area again. I would frequently find them where I had only passed an hour or so before. Heavens knows where they had been!

At this time, Mother had a possible buyer for the bungalow. Although I wanted to move, if there was a chance of buying a place with a good many acres of ground in our area, I wanted to stay local. Mother would only look at properties that were miles away, and not where my sister or I wanted live. It was a waste of time looking at properties with one or two acres. Whenever she did look at a bigger place with a lot of acreage, she would be guided by what other people said, including my older brother Brian. Just to make things worse, he would always go with Mother to look at the properties. What could one do at 15 years old - not a lot one might say! This situation had been going on for quite a while, and myself and my sister Christine were glad when we were told that our buyer had given up waiting for Mother to find a suitable place.

My other brother Geoffrey, who was 19 then, was also interested in the possibility of us getting a farm. We thought that we would get a farm in Somerset, but that never did come to anything. She kept in touch with the estate agent in Somerset for some four years. When I was old enough to drive, we went down to Minehead and met the estate agent who had been sending us details of properties for a few years, but it never did come to anything. Just wasn't meant to be, I guess.

The same time that our place was up for sale, the two properties next door either side of us were up for sale too. I tried to get Mother interested in buying one side, because the seven acres were attached to our place some years earlier and a bungalow was built on this ground in 1958. But Mother showed no interest in buying the place, as she wanted to move right away. She missed a very good chance of getting something bigger. This place had seven acres, a new bungalow and outbuildings for seven tie-up cow pens. If only we had bought the place, perhaps by the time I was 20 years old we might have built up a small herd ready to take on a bigger farm. But, as always, we never got the chance. The property sold a few months later for £5,000 and it had a milk round to go with it! At that time our place was only worth £2,500 and we had one acre of ground and outbuildings.

This uncertainty continued right up until the New Year in 1960, when Mother finally settled on a place, being in a state of panic. The place was in Newbury, Berkshire, and not having transport, it wasn't very easy for us to go and see. Knowing Mother as well as I did, she would take us to a dump of a place! With all this dragging on for so long it was beginning to get us down. Mid-January 1960, I travelled to Newbury on the back of my brother's scooter. It was a freezing cold Sunday, and I hadn't dressed against the cold, so I froze. The house was run down and would have needed a lot of money spent on it. Why Mother made another silly choice in her life, not letting the rest of us know how we felt and not listening to her family, except my older brother Brian…he would have gone along with anything, as Christine and I saw it. At that time there was very little prospect of work there, and the place only had one acre of ground, so we would have been even worse off, because there would have been no forest rights there. Brian thought like Mother and agreed with her that the place could be done up. So it could have been. If I remember right, it was on the market for £1,500. I think Mother was thinking that with the bit of spare cash left over, we could have bought some more cows, but that would have been a waste of time as the place was too small. By the time we got home that Sunday afternoon, I was feeling even more down than before I went. I could see even less prospect of ever getting a farm with a good acreage of our own if this sale went through. It dragged on for another two months, before it all fell through, but before it all came to an end, I really thought about staying behind. I was offered a caravan over at the farm, which I wasn't too keen on at the time but may have been glad of it if the sale had gone through. I had had enough of Mother's silly ideas.

Despite all these goings on, Geoffrey and I dug out the bank, with the idea of putting a circular drive in. We laid it through our paddock, so that when we had a vehicle it would make it easier for parking, and perhaps for unloading hay and straw. But having another gateway and not having a proper gate to put up, it was an open invitation for all the forest ponies to get in and eat our grass when we didn't have very much for our own cows. It had been a lot of hard work for nothing, digging out the bank in the first place. In the end it was put back in its regional bank. I was glad see it put back. Geoffrey, who had left home, saw that the idea and our effort had been a waste of time. At least no more ponies and another people's cattle could get back in at night, as had so often happened - we had been getting up one or two o'clock in the morning to drive them out so we could get some sleep. With the dogs barking as well, it was bedlam sometimes.

Summer 1959 was a good time for rearing calves for beef as a good price was being paid that year. We used to buy calves when they were a few days old, at about £6-7 each for a Friesian, weaned them from their mothers, then put them on to feed from one of our cows, Alex, who was a very good foster mother to the calves. We then sent them on to Ringwood market four or five weeks later and usually doubled our money. But it was all in vain because by the time Winter came around again, there was never any feed for the cows. Mother never put the money back in to the farming side of the business, so invariably the cows went hungry and got into a poor state, very thin and boney. For me it was a dreadful sight to see each year after working hard through the Summer and Mother never giving a thought about the Winter to come. Sometimes I used to buy in hay and straw for them so the animals wouldn't go hungry; by the time another Summer arrived, all would be forgotten until the next Winter.

That same year I needed a new bike, so I bought one through a club at the Co-op in Ringwood. I only had it a few months and practically wrecked it. I used to like riding it fast up the lane and over the bumps in the Drove. Once I took the corner coming into the Drove too fast, and came off, breaking the handlebars. I didn't know whether I contributed to them breaking off or there was a fault in the metal. Anyway, the bike was returned, and new handlebars were fitted. After this episode, I rode the bike properly and took care with it, and it lasted me right until 1965, when I sold it for a £1. The bike cost me £15 in 1959.

Being my first year in full time work, when it came to hay making time it was quite hard going handling thousands of bales of hay. With no big hay barns in those days, all the hay had to be taken to various places, such as to the hut down the Drove. Today most of the huts have gone along the Drove. It was hard going. All the bales had to be unloaded, then carried one by one, with no more than two people at a time to carry them as we would get in each other's way. What used to make it harder was the brick work at the entrance, which was very narrow, so the bales had to be virtually dragged around the corner and carried right down to the other end of the hut. Throughout the day, the hut filled up with bales of hay with the heat from the sun beaming on the corrugated tin. It made the place very hot to work in. This way of storing the bales only went on for a few more years after which they built a big barn where they could stack all the hay.

Come the Wintertime, when all the bales had to be carried back to the farm, our work commenced in reverse order. The bales had to be carried back and put onto the elevator then loaded onto the trailer. The biggest trailer at that time carried 250 bales of hay. The worse part for me was having to bring the bales out of the hut, because the place was infected with rats and they didn't run away either which made it worse. As I couldn't stand the look of them, I would drag a bale out slowly, fearing they might come at me. In the end, Clive realised I feared the rats, and he put the bales of hay onto the elevator and I loaded them. When the bales of hay had been loaded, the trailer was taken back to the farm and placed inside the barn and offloaded as and when needed. Usually 20 bales were needed every day. Being a long cow pen of 80, 20 tie-up bales were carried down the long cow pen, one at a time, and dropped over the wall. Then all the strings had to be cut and collected up, which was what I used to do during my working years at the farm. Then some hay was put into the cow pen troughs, ready for cows to eat during their milking time. This had to be done every day of the week during the Winter months but this method came to an end some five years later when the milking parlour replaced the cow pen, and there was no time for the cows to eat hay, just enough time to eat cattle cake while they were being milked.

Another job which used to be hard going was the unloading of the cattle cake, which was usually delivered once a month by lorry, five tonnes at a time. The cake had to be taken off the lorry and put on an old disused cart; once drawn by a horse, the cart was very useful for storing the bags of cattle cake which used to weigh one and a quarter hundred weight each. Then it was tipped into a barrow and pushed up the cow pen and weighed to the appropriate amount to be given each cow, according to the amount of milk the cow produced. Today all this is done automatically by setting the number on the dial of the machine for the amount needed for each cow, which saves cake and a lot of time when milking. The other big difference regarding the handling of cake is that now it arrives lose on a lorry and then it is blown into a big hopper, which usually stands behind the diary, and is fed automatically through to the parlour for the cows, cutting out all the handling of tonnes of cattle cake.

The one thing that I will always remember that Summer, was during haymaking time. I worked one Sunday all day for 7 hours. I started off by helping to milk the cows, then loading bales of hay (it seemed like hundreds that day) for only 15 shillings. It always seemed unfair to only get a quarter of what an adult received for doing the same job. Later that Summer, another lad, Buster Sharad as he was known, came to work at the farm. Being the same age, we got on very well. We used to try out all the brands of cigarettes together. After trying them all, I stopped smoking altogether as they cost me 2/6 for 20. I found that it was costing me over 8 shillings a week, which was a lot out of £2. Buster didn't have to pay quite so much at home, so he was able to afford to smoke. By the end of January 1960, he left the farm and went to work for the Council.

By this time, Terry had left school, and he got a job looking after broiler chickens, as they were called, imported from America. You could buy one thousand chicks for £50 and rear them in about seven to eight weeks. They spent most of their lifetime in semi-darkness, and at the end of the eight weeks they were put into crates. All this happened at 5am In the morning. It had to be that early because they had to be at the factory before the staff arrived. We used to do this right through the Summer, over the Drove as well. Terry and I used to clean out the huts in the evenings and we were paid £3 each.

By Spring 1960, the sale on the house had finally fallen through and it was a great relief, for me in particular. Also in 1960, Mother bought another Alsatian bitch, Becky. She was black and again she was fully grown, but although she was friendly, she was untrained and couldn't be let off the lead, so I put up a run for the dogs using the air-raid shelter for them to sleep in.

By the end of 1960 I had left the farm and went out on my own doing gardening. But not knowing very much about it made it hard going, and my heart being in full-time farming made it worse. That year my brother Geoffrey left home as well. It was sad at first, but better for all of us because there were always fights breaking out between us. But he did come back for a while the following year. On my travels around the area I ended up working over at Linwood and seeing a lot of Terry, which was good because we always got on well and we used to go out socially too. Later on, in 1961, I found myself working for a Mr. Atkins who I got on very well with. He managed to stay in the broiler business when others just had to give up. His buildings only consisted of wire post frames with straw pushed down in between the two sets of wire mesh - a good idea, but the straw was always falling out and had to be refilled with new straw. This is where I came in doing just that for some time, earning three shillings per hour.

1961

In the early part of 1961 I found myself milking cows again in the mornings at Wyatt's Farm. It only lasted until Mr. Wyatt's son had got over his operation. I enjoyed doing it very much, milking the cows with a machine rather than hand milking which I didn't care for. Having that job for the early part of the year gave me a lot of time at home during the day, and I was able to tidy the place up which I always did. By this time we had virtually finished with pigs as the market for them had gone down and it all came to a sudden end. After this we had a Nissen hut erected, installed a good concrete base with proper drainage and in here we kept a couple of pigs with the calves. All the old pig stays were knocked down and the rubble ended up being used to fill in the big potholes in the Drove; tonnes were put in. Today the potholes are still the same, even worse. Each pothole would take 3 to 4 tonnes of rubble to fill it in, so you can see I have been missed for the last 20 years! But I am sometimes back up there again, filling them in with rubble from other places.

While all this was going on in 1961, we were pressing ahead to get a Dairy License so we could send our own milk away. But we were turned down on the grounds of only having well water, which in their eyes wasn't suitable for cooling the milk or anything else. The well was almost outside our door, just a few feet away. When it rained, all the water used to run straight into it. The cause of all this was the lorries running over the manhole and it always getting broken. Before the year was out, the West Hampshire Water Company put mains water down and we were connected soon after, but strangely enough, we didn't get the license for our Dairy until July 1962, when we finally started sending milk away. It was a lot of hard work. Usually you had to have two churns; one for the night's milk and one for the morning, so that meant walking down to the bottom of the Drove twice as only one churn would fit into the wheelbarrow. This went on for nearly two years. When there wasn't very much milk, I used to mix it - providing it was cooled well it was ok. It saved me a lot of running about for nothing. Really it all came too late. I could see there was no future doing is this way.

It was hopeless really in the beginning of 1961. We lost one of the cows, partly from it eating too many potatoes and she being underfed in the first place. She didn't get over it and had to be shot and taken to the knacker's yard, for dog's meat no doubt. We lost so many like this. Our best cow Hopey had gone at the beginning of 1963 as well, because her hoof had got twisted. Our cows did too much walking for cows in milk – it's a wonder they gave any milk at all with all the miles they walked to find a bit of food.

By April 1961, the broiler chicken business came to an end, so Terry finished there and went over to Linwood to another farm and just about did everything from milking cows to ploughing fields up. He was there until 1984 when he finally left and went out on his own doing contract work.

1962

By Easter 1962 my sister Christine had left school and didn't have a job to start with. She was keen on hairdressing, so Mother tried to get her in at various places, but it cost too much for the training. There was no help in those days, or if there was, we didn't know about it! So, she, like so many, didn't have a proper job to go to. She helped me a lot with the animals and even taking the milk down in the wheelbarrow which was a great help for me. Later that year, thousands of poultry at Manor Farm got fowl pest and all the chickens had to be destroyed. The owner, Mr. Gibb, sold the farm to a Mr. Parnell, but they didn't know anything about farming and suffered even bigger losses. However, before that happened, Christine got a job there looking after the chickens and collecting the eggs.

By the beginning of that 1962 I decided I would tackle our air-raid shelter that was built beside the bungalow to protect the occupier during the Second World War. As well as remembering what it was put there for and the good times we had as children playing on the top of it, I always looked at it as being an eyesore, so I decided it would be a challenge to knock it down and clear it away. I set about it knocking the roof in first. That was the easy part. Barrow loads of rubble had to be wheeled down to the bottom of the Drove to fill in in the potholes – there were plenty of them as well. Some three months later, the whole lot was cleared away. At Easter time we had a French student staying with us and he didn't mind helping me move the stuff away. With all the steel rods through the brick walls, it took a lot of stamina to keep at it at the age of seventeen.

Aunt Peggy, Christine and Greta

While all this was going on, I started driving lessons throughout the Winter and Spring and part of the Summer months. I passed after the third attempt on the 22nd August 1962. Lessons cost me £1 per hour - in those days I still had to work 5 o 6 hours to get £1. Again, it was hard going being self-employed, because no job was ever guaranteed, so it was all the more difficult to pay for the driving lessons. However, I managed to get through as most do. I had beaten my older brother Geoffrey to passing his driving test, and he was four years older than me, so I felt it was good going. He passed in January 1963. My older brother Brian had passed his test in 1961 through British Railways, as it was known then. But we all used to take the mickey, by saying that he only had to drive round the Goods Yard, and that was good enough, because they were very short of lorry drivers. By this time the ground where the air-raid shelter had been was finally cleared away and planted out with potatoes and later put down to grass.

By 1962 I had my first car; it was a 1952 Vauxhall Wyvern and I started driving it around to look for the cows in it. But that was difficult and expensive too, even for those days. It made it a lot easier for getting round quicker to be in the car looking for the cows, rather than cycling miles in all weathers, but not so much when you had to stop and start, and get in and out of the car to drive the cows on. If you didn't, the cows would start grazing any nice grass they came across and it took even longer in the end. I didn't use the car again for that purpose.

September that year I was offered a job at Woolley and Wallis on market day (Wednesday) at £2 for the day. At that time Geoffrey, my brother, was working there full-time. I only stayed a month before being offered a building job working at Avon Castle and Woolsbridge Road. I took the job on full-time for £12 per week. Not having very many gardening jobs then to do, didn't matter too much that I had taken this job on. But as the Winter progressed it became very cold and miserable. However, in the New Year of 1963, with roads being icy and snowed up most of the time, it was a great experience for me being my actual first Winter of driving on my own. As there was no building work going on at the time, there was a lot of clearing to do, mainly Rhododendrons. We were able to keep warm during the very cold weather, because of the burning up of the wood and a lot of heat came from the fires. Despite the frozen snow, it all melted and burned. The clearing work was very tiring because of the amount of snow we had to plod through all day. Luckily, I kept the cows this Winter, so it made it easier for me to milk at night and in the morning, but it was hard going getting to work by 8am. Today some 22 years later, where we were clearing is all built on with large gardens and surrounded by lots of pine trees, making good use of the ground which couldn't be used for much else. I helped to landscape a lot of the gardens and clear the grounds.

By mid-February I was becoming unsettled. The people I worked with were not easy to get along with - one needed to in order to stick the harsh kind of conditions that had to be endured. Really, it wasn't for me. Then by chance, I was asked if I would like to take a job back at Hucklesbrook Farm, back in the Dairy milking the cows. I had only left three years previously when I worked alongside Clive, Mr. Sampson's eldest son. After we had come to an agreement over wages, I gave notice to the building site. I had done just about everything in the short time I was there; from being a Chippy's mate to a builders' Labourer, and anything else that was asked of me. Being a small firm, you had to be willing to do most things. It was interesting while it lasted but I hated it, at the same time, and wasn't sorry when it came to an end. Even so, it helped me through the Winter and paid my way, particularly having my own car to pay for with payments of £10 per month.

Going back on the farm full-time brought my reign of being self-employed to an end after nearly 2 and a half years, and with a guaranteed wage of £13 per week and some of my gardening jobs reappearing after the long Winter, I was earning £15 or £16 per week. So by early April 1963, I was able to improve the age of my car by 10 years by selling the 1952 Vauxhall Wyvern for £80 and putting it towards a 1962 Ford Consul. It was touch and go whether I could get the deposit in time, but with Mother's help I managed to raise the cash needed, which was £40. I felt as if I was on top of the world. I had always wanted a decent car, like most people of that time. It came quite early for me I suppose but I had worked for it through the cold Winter doing a miserable job I hated. 1962 I found myself working quite happily, doing a job that I liked. I was up early in the mornings, which I also liked, but at the same time I usually found myself scraping in just after 6.15am or later; as always, never getting anywhere on time, not even for the cows.

Me with Ford Consul

By the late Summer I was able to enjoy a week's holiday. At the same time, Mother had her very close friend and children down to stay from London who always liked the country life. Because her children were boys, I got on with them very well, particularly where the animals were concerned. So, having that week off while they were down here, we set off to Somerset for the day, arriving in the town of Minehead. We got there by 8am with Mother's old trick of putting the clocks on a good hour or so. We must have left home by 4.30 to have got there at that time and the rest of them slept on the way. The idea behind the trip, I discovered, was to see the estate agent who Mother had been in touch with for many years, regarding farms in the area, as mentioned earlier in the story, but nothing came of it so that was the end of that.

With it being a wet Summer, harvest time was a lot easier this year at the Farm. This was the first year they had a combine harvester, so there wasn't any corn or barley to be ricked. I was still keeping the gardening jobs going as having every Saturday off enabled me to do other jobs on Saturday mornings. This also included working up at the poultry farm to help my sister with the chickens.

For the eight months I was working at the farm, I also had to endure a lot of hassle from the chaps who I had worked with before. I suppose I must have looked to them as being up on a pedestal, having the job offered to me when there was a lad of a similar age who wasn't offered the job in the dairy who they felt wasn't suitable. He never did take up the position, even after I had to finish later. One particular chap, who had worked at the farm for years and had very little himself, used to make mischief between us, probably as I was the only one at that time who had a decent car, and it was the same type of car as the bosses, Mr. Sampson. That didn't go down too well with the other chaps. One thing is clear writing this 20 years later, it doesn't matter what you do or where you go, there will be someone who will try and make life difficult for you. That's my opinion of this life so far.

With the Summer gradually coming to an end and Winter in sight again, it had been a very happy time for me, despite the difficulties with the others. I shall always remember crossing the fields early in the mornings! With the sensational music of that time, I had become interested enough to want to buy an electric guitar and amplifier to go with it, and being keen, I bought one second-hand costing £50, paid in cash that left me broke just about. I thought I would have the £10.10s to fall back on, being in a steady job, but instead soon found myself with no job. I turned up as normal on the Monday morning, having already worked on the Sunday. Everything seemed okay, however that morning I was told that I would no longer be needed. Mr. Sampson informed me himself. Looking back to that time, Clive was unusually quiet that morning - it soon became clear why! It was a sad day walking across the fields for the last time. It seemed once again that farming and working with dairy cows had gone forever.

I was to receive one month's wages but with Mother owing them money for hay and straw, I didn't receive that either. I was too easy going and just accepted it, but I should have received the £42 by rights, in spite of what was owing to them. But being loyal to my Mother, I let it go. It just meant that I didn't have to pay my way at home for a while, but this didn't help me too much because I had my car to pay for. Luckily I had paid extra payments in the hope of paying it off earlier, but that went by the wayside. On top of my problems, I was continually threatened by Mother that as she had signed the Higher Purchase forms, the car was hers. Even so, I had been paying for it at £15 per month. This always came up whenever Mother wanted things her way, until one day I had had enough of being threatened in this way; I said, if you want the car, take it and take the payments on as well. After I said that, I was never threatened again in that way.

1963-64

By this time, 1963, we were finally down to two cows: Bubbles and Honeybell, the last calf I reared to a milking cow. We were able to keep them in the paddock as were sending less milk away to the milk marketing board. By early November 1963 I was offered a job up at the poultry farm where my sister was working, which I accepted as there wasn't anything else going at the time and it was close to home as well. When I took the job on there were so many other people working there and doing very little. The owners had started to realise just how many extras they had working for them, and that they were not getting very much in return for their money. They had one chap supposed to building an extension on the house and helping-out on the farm. He and I soon fell out – over a wheelbarrow! He never did what I would call work. After our set-to, Mrs. Pernell told him he would no longer be required, so that was the end of that. Gradually there were less and less people working there. Just my sister and I were left in the end, and a couple of lads who came on Saturdays to help-out in the morning to put the chicken food round for the week. I was able to use the Land Rover to carry the food stuff around the place.

By April 1964 my sister Christine decided to leave the poultry farm and work at the International Store in Ringwood - it had not long changed over to self-service when she went there. That left me on my own. They intended to take another replacement after my sister left. But by June 1964 I decided I didn't see why I should be working for the same wage, covering almost all the work that took two of us and sometimes three. I worked a 50-hour week for £13 per week. Also, as part of the working week, I delivered bags of chicken manure, driving the Land Rover to make the delivery in the Bournemouth area for the £6-7 per bag which they received. I bagged this up with my sister's help on her half day off on a Thursday afternoon. On Fridays I used to clean the Land Rover too. I was a good allrounder. I thought it not to be unreasonable to ask for £15 per week for a 45-hour week, but they turned it down, saying that they couldn't afford to pay the extra. What extra I ask? They were paying out less anyway, and I was reliable too. But that was that.

I loved farming but I guess in those days maybe it was seen as normal to only pay the minimum rate, no matter how good you were at the job, or what they saved. Some years later I set up in my own business as a Landscape Gardener and have been self-employed for 39 years and still going. That Summer, during the hay making season, I only worked driving the tractor, turning the already cut hay over and putting one line of hay into another ready for bailing. The job was in Alderholt and paid six shillings an hour. 1964 was a hot Summer as I recall. At Harvest time, in early August, I mainly carted bales of straw from the fields to the barn. In between I continued looking after the chickens. They were housed in a big place. I had to put chicken feed in their troughs, collect the eggs and do odd jobs about the place, but the owner was never satisfied. I found him a miserable so and so and regretted having to leave the farm as I always seemed to make one bad move after another. However, there was no choice; as always, I stuck it out. To make it worse, the owner took a shilling an hour off my wages, so I was back to the same money I was on before I left Manor Farm, plus having to use the car every day cost me in petrol - another error I had made.

By this time my sister asked me if I wanted to go out with one of the girls from the shop that she was working with. At first I said I didn't, this being a blind date, but changed my mind later! The person I met on the following Saturday night was to become my wife, 19 months later and for 19 years of marriage. While we were getting to know each other, someone asked me if we would sell or rent our paddock. Like everything else I do, I said the place was still for sale. Within five months, the place was sold for £5.100 to Lady Grant Lawson who bought the place for her gardener.

At first it seemed an exciting prospect, buying a good size property. But Mother again wouldn't go for anything of any size, instead looking at a small holding at Four Marks near Alton. All this consisted of was 10 acres. At the time of viewing the property, the owner told us that we could rent a further 20 acres, but as Mother hadn't followed it up through the solicitors, this property was taken for the asking price when we could have got it for less. We discovered that one field wasn't for renting and we didn't know who the other one belonged to. At the time, I was still over at Alderholt carting straw but towards the end of August 1964, the job just came to an end just like that. So I had a spell of being without a job for a while, although still doing some gardening jobs which I carried on with. By this time, my older brother kept badgering me to join British Railways. I wasn't keen on the idea as my heart was in farming and I still hoped, with all the extreme effort I had put in, to possibly own and run our own dairy herd of cows one day. I decided to give it a try, starting at Ringwood Station by mid-September. Betty and I were going steady by this time.

Before I took the job on the railway, I tried a milk round job, having to start at 5am in the morning and in 1964 you had to be there on time. That was something I wasn't used to doing. After being told by the manager that I would last five minutes if I couldn't get there on time, I decided that the job wasn't for me either, so I gave it up no sooner than starting it, £15 per week or no £15. The job on the railways was paying £8 for a 44-hour week, with overtime at 2 hours from five to seven in the evening. It meant I would take home £10.10s per week. With only bus fares, instead of buying petrol and saving the wear and tear on the car, this was quite a saving and lasted me a couple of months, after which I was to experience higher running costs on the car for a few months to come. One of the jobs I used to do at Ringwood Railway Station Goods Yard was to tie down very large Mack Slurry Spreaders, delivered by Wright Rains Tractors, which produced these great slurry spreaders sent all over the country. Once again for me - a connection with farming.

Thursday 12th November 1964 - 13 years to the day that we moved there – was another sad time for me as we left our place at Ibsley Drove and the lovely surroundings after so many years. It was the end of an era on that Thursday, I remember so well. I left them to it, Mother and my eldest brother, to get on with packing. Mother telephoned the Railway Station at Ringwood, where I was working at the time. After speaking to me to tell me I should come home and help out, I told her I was at work and I was staying there. I said it was her idea to move and she never consulted me or my sister Christine (my eldest brother Brian was my Mother's favourite). At the end of the working day, I went back to Ibsley Drove to be in Forest View once more, in this place for the last time, and felt very emotional, being the kind of person that I am; I fall in love with places, even when I was only nearly seven years old when I accrued the same emotions. It was bad enough having to leave our colonial-style bungalow at Kedge Anchor, Wraysbury, and that wonderful view we had looking at Windsor Castle, without knowing this would have the same effect on me later in life, whether in this country or in foreign lands. After spending a little time thinking about all the amazing things that happened while we lived here, and how we farmed all the animals, and all the good people we got to know and liked and in lots of cases good friends too, I left there with a heavy heart and made my way to our new home, Woodlea Farm.

I decided after being at Woodlea Farm for only a few days that I wasn't going to stay. I decided to go back to Ringwood Railway station and get my job back, which I did after speaking with the Station Master, Mr. Henbest, subject to being able to find lodgings suitable to me. Of course, I didn't find any, and my wife to be didn't know of any either. As I didn't mention it to anyone other than Betty, I just carried on where I was living at the new home on Woodlea Farm. It cost me 15 shillings per 100 miles or so for petrol in my car, and with no cash flow coming my way, as I led Mother to believe. I also worked hard on getting the new place cleaned up. When I rejoined the Railway, at the time there was a job going at Alton Station Goods Yard, unloading and loading wagons, something I was familiar with, which I applied for and got in December 1964. But in April 1965, the Goods Yard closed. I was offered a Porter's job on the platform at Alton Railway Station, and that meant shift work, something I had never done before. This entailed a week's training course at Wimbledon learning to assist passengers, dividing electric trains and Railway Operations, which I liked doing. I passed the exam I learned later. I was also offered the job on overtime to refill the oil lamps for the signals in station limits which I did do. The outer limit signal was very high to climb but I made it many times, after the first climb, to near the top of the signal. I used to transfer boxes of Watercress from the Southampton train to the trains bound for London. I also used to have the job of releasing baskets full of tamed pigeons - after being released they would fly back to where they lived. I liked doing that too.

It seemed quite good to start with, working 6am to 3.30pm or 3.30pm until midnight. Being an electrified line to Waterloo, and a service every half hour, it made the job more interesting to see more people wanting to travel on the trains with the better service provided.

1965

By February 1965, Betty and I decided to get engaged. When I told Mother of my intentions, she became most upset by the whole affair, and she even thought I would give up going to and from home to see Betty. I was to marry in Ringwood, later that year. With no prospect of farming, Mother wasn't serious in doing anything other than expecting me to keep the place tidy and saw up wood for the fire. Ten acres and still only two cows - all the grass had become overgrown - and we could get no further with getting any more cows. My sister and I asked why Mother bothered coming to live here. We had taken in lodgers to help keep the place going, so it wasn't too great at home, plus we had a caravan up beside our drive and that was let as well to bring in a few pounds. But it never made any difference to the farm side or me, and Brian never did anything to help-out in the way of keeping the place tidy. So, as things seemed to get worse and worse between myself and Mother, by September that year, Betty and I had fixed a date to marry - October 30th. Arrangements had to be made of course, regarding where I was going to work and transfer to.

I had put in for a job at Bournemouth Railway Station for a shunters position, which entailed dividing steam train coaches and detaching steam engines, as they still were then. After deciding what I was going to do, we had to find a flat, something I wasn't looking forward to or never dreamed of doing. It tended to make me miserable thinking about the future and knowing that maybe it was the end of farming for me. After weeks of looking for a flat in Bournemouth, we finally came across one in Oxford Road, which was walking distance to Bournemouth Railway Station, my new place of work. The rent for the flat was £4.10s per week.

By mid-October I finally decided to leave home, and Mother being in her usual style when things weren't going her way, just wouldn't speak to me. I didn't say goodbye. I said to myself: "Well that's that".

The wedding took place on the 30th October 1965 with Mother not attending as expected. My older brother Brian didn't come either - we suspected he didn't want to offend Mother. My brother Geoffrey and sister Christine were actually the only two from my side of the family who came; the rest were friends and Betty's side of the family. Betty, my wife, had lost her mother when she was 12 years old, and her father just 7 years later. After the wedding we flew to Jersey for a week, taking off from Hurn Airport. What a time of year to get married! Pitch black, wet at the time and cold. I wouldn't pick that time of year if I were ever to do it again! But we had a good week in Jersey, costing £13 each for the flight there and back, and £14 for the two of us at a guest house. But what a journey we had coming back! Having arrived at Jersey Airport late, we missed the flight back to Hurn Airport, so we had to take a flight on a 1.11 jet airline to Gatwick and take a train into London. It took hours to get back - 3 hours from London to Bournemouth in those days; even the fastest train took two hours. Then we had to get a bus to Hurn Airport and being a Saturday afternoon, it was a long wait to pick up my car - it took all day and it spoiled a good week.

And I wasn't looking forward to working at the station, particularly with steam engines. It was in November too - another new challenge for me to overcome, which I soon did. After Sunday off, it was down to Bournemouth Railway Station. There were only a couple of people my age group, in their early 20s, all the rest were their 40s and 50s. Almost all those people I worked with then have sadly passed. The station was badly run and so many were employed. I'd had weeks of training in this job but certainly didn't feel like rushing to take the job on, especially as it was run in an army-style. I was always being chased by the Station Manager if he saw me not wearing the silly cap. I was so determined that I wasn't going to wear one, that I used to change turns and kept out of the way of anyone who said anything about wearing it; I never did, and neither did the other chaps that took on the newly created shunting positions when the electric trains came in to full service on 10th July 1967.

By Christmas 1965 I decided to take a flight, and we flew up to the north from Southampton Airport. Being my father-in-law's first flight, it was quite exciting for him and us. It was the second time for Betty and me. I thought it would be a good idea to go on holiday over the Christmas period. I had no idea how the traffic side of the railway was run at that time. It was an hour's flight to Manchester Ringway Airport, as it was known then. It took one hour to get from the Airport to my wife's sister's place. With a similar journey back, and very cold, we arrived back home and into the New Year: 1966.

The job was going steady and I was able to save £4 per week towards a house, or whatever. I didn't want Betty to go out to work - that way I knew how much cash I had left out of my weekly income to meet a future mortgage, and I liked her being home as I came home at different times of the day. The one thing I disliked about living in a flat was not being able to put my car in a driveway; instead it had to be parked on the roadside. Luckily for me, the people next door very kindly let me park my car on their drive, so it was off the road.

1966

By March 1966, changes were on the way with the electrification of trains coming soon. I was one step ahead of the older chaps who had no experience of electric trains. A lot of them were frightened by the thought of electrification and having to get underneath trains with the third rail there, I remember them saying at the time. I had learned, just about, where the lines went to and where all the points were. You had to know where all the points were inside station limits, in order to know which ground signal controlled them. All the signals were oil lit at that time and it was terrible to see by properly, day or night. The semaphore signals were the same, oil lit, and invariably you had a job to see them because the glass was faded and smoke and grease prevented them from reflecting the light very well. So it was much harder for me, not being used to it, and not wanting to make any mistakes either. But at least the semaphore signals were on a gantry very high up, so you could see the signal when it was pulled off from a distance. It was my guess that all the ground and semaphore signals were all going to be changed to a coloured system pretty soon (in the year of 1966).

I found myself being taken over the ground of the station limits by the Inspector, and I had learned more than I thought and remembered it as well. Even so I had been told by one of the relief chaps, who was supposedly teaching me the job, that I would never make the grade. He actually said something else which isn't repeatable! I laughed. He didn't know me very well. If he had known me some 14 years earlier, he would have known what a tough life I had long before I joined British Rail. Anyway, he worked 12 hours so didn't want chaps like me taking on the job. It's the same old story whenever young people appear on a job - you were always told that you wouldn't be any good. It did apply to some of course, but it didn't apply to me because I wasn't going to let it, just because I hadn't worked with steam engines.

The relief's shunters were sent to other stations and not seen again, and one left so that made three positions vacant, one of which I filled. Another lad younger than me did the same. You had to be 18 years old before you could take the job on. The job was worth an extra £2 per week, taking my basic to 263 shillings for a 44 hour a week. But with a threatened strike and a complete shutdown of the station, we ended up with a shorter working week and we were on a 40-hour week shortly after. As always, there was never enough staff to fill every position, so there was a lot of overtime being worked, mainly 12 hours per day or night. I remember doing the very first night turn. Working through the night was no fun, having never done it before, but once I had done it a few times, it wasn't too bad. But I never did it by choice. It used to make me very miserable sometimes, seeing everyone going home and I was just starting at 6pm in the evening. The good thing about it for me, was if I ever did any Portering, or whatever, I was paid at my own rate. Even so, I didn't care too much for all the overtime, although it was helping me to save quite a lot of money each week through the Railways Bank. The money was taken out for me. I was determined that I was going to buy my own place sooner or later and move out of the flat.

After a couple of months, the other two positions were filled by a couple of chaps of a similar age. The younger one mentioned earlier, who was 18 at the time, had to give the job up as he was overweight and couldn't get in between the trains very well and we only had a few minutes to divide the trains. So that was Bill's shunting career over, but he became a good friend. This other chap, Brian, I got on very well with. He was very helpful when the job got difficult as he had more experience than me. The other position was covered temporarily by a chap called Charlie, who was waiting to take a 'carriage and wagon' job, as it was known then.

At this time, we used to go down to see Mr. and Mrs. Richards quite a lot at Ibsley Drove. On one occasion, we took them to Portsmouth for the day, as they didn't have a car and they were good friends. We had got to know them having lived down the Drove at a similar time as we did. I still missed where we lived. It was a good day out in Portsmouth, seeing the Victory for the first time, and afterwards I had my first rest day off, which we weren't entitled to before the 40-hour week came about. On the way back, Mrs. Richards suggested we call in on Mother, as she was a friend of hers when we lived in Ibsley Drove. It seemed quite a good idea, thinking things might have changed somewhat. Well, we arrived at Woodlea Farm in the dark. Mr. and Mrs. Richards went in first and we were quite well received. Mother was one of those people that you could have crossed swords with, and later you would think nothing had happened. I hadn't spoken to her for over six months. I still thought I was in with a chance regarding the farm. By now, the place had gone back to dilapidated chicken sheds and overgrown fields - problems that I had encountered with Mother over the years. I still had more interest than Brian, my older brother, ever did and it seemed such a shame to see the place looking a mess after my hard work the previous year. Brian wasn`t concerned at all. He spent a lot of time at the signal box at Four Marks Station, across the fields from where he lived. He had known the signalmen since he had moved there in 1964. Later that year, the Four Marks Station was closed and a ticket collector was put on the trains instead of staffing the station.

Alsation at Four Marks Station

After the last visit we went to visit Mother and Woodlea Farm quite regularly. It made a nice change from the flat. In 1966, due to the electrification of the Bournemouth line, all the main line trains were diverted via Alton through Four Marks, and on to the main line at Winchester junction. It was a good change and it showed how useful the line really was. My sister Christine had planned to marry that year, but that was called off. I wouldn't have been surprised if it was Mother who had put her off. Sadly, she decided not to have any children and I had the same Idea. Thank heavens my wife had a different idea. My sister was very good at helping me out on the farm, with the cows or pigs for that matter at feeding time, or just helping-out in general as Christine and I shared the same dream of being with animals. By the Summer of 1966, I was wondering how I could buy a farm myself. There was a farm with 100 acres near Devon, priced at £10,000 which I was interested in, but with little chance of raising that kind of money, and not having any myself, I didn't think I had a very good chance. So that's the way it went.

By 1969 prices had risen considerably. A small holding of 17 acres near Ropley, Hampshire was for sale at £12,500. It consisted of a farm building, a dairy and a big hay barn. At the time I had an extraordinarily helpful accountant who helped me look into buying it. I shall never forget his help. However, it was never to materialise. All the time I was working at Bournemouth Railway Station I hoped to have a small holding of my own. With another two years to go before being able to buy a bungalow, in 1968, I still had a lot of hard saving for a deposit to do. I went to Lloyds Bank to try and raise £5,000 towards the cost of buying 24 Friesian cows and a tractor. The Ropley farm already had a lot of farm implements to be going on with, but I would only have had £3,000 left over from the bungalow had it gone through, and still fell short. Twenty-four cows would have cost £2,500 and a monthly milk cheque would have been roughly £120 - it just wasn't enough to pay for the farm mortgage and the loan from the bank. This is how the bank manager saw it. Had the chance been taken by both sides, meaning had the bank been prepared to lend the money needed, I might have made it. But some two years later, the prices of property shot up beyond all recognition and put an end to the possibility of me ever owning a farm. It was out of my reach forever.

Most of the extra savings had to come from working overtime, which usually meant working 12 hours most working days. Working the extra hours most weeks, in and out, meant doing part of another shift, which usually involved a lot of shunting parcel train vans, plus taking empty rolling stock down to the sidings for other services. In most cases, this was done in the dark, with no lights in the sidings in those days and only a little oil lamp, which if dropped, would go out on you. The shunter carried the oil lamp to convey a signal to the driver and his fireman, as to which side of the train you had to work from. I was in charge of all movements once the train was in the sidings short of the stopping block. The train was then was divided for the early morning services. One of the things I used to do to get around losing sight of the driver, when bringing the trains back in the sidings in the dark, was to jump off the train so the driver could see my lamp signal better. Luckily, I didn't have any mishaps.

In 1966 we saw the end of the Somerset and Dorset line from Bournemouth to Bath. British Rail Temple Meads station also remained closed right until 1983 – it was 17 years before any trains stopped there again, when the line was electrified. After a year, Bournemouth West was finally closed as a main line terminus station in 1965 and was only used as a carriage siding as it always had done before the closure of the station. All the services were transferred to Bournemouth Station. The fast trains were every two hours in those days. The make-up of the stock was different from today regarding the movement of the trains. In those days, the 'West Portion', as it was known, would run in engine detached coaches, and a shunting engine came on the other end ready to pull back into the sidings. The passengers used to board the trains, and when it was about to be shunted into the sidings most people thought that the train was leaving, waving goodbye even after it had been announced that the train had to be shunted so that the Weymouth portion could be run in. The rear part of the train which had been shunted to the sidings, would be attached to the Weymouth portion, and still people would wave goodbye even after they had been told that the train was coming back. The hardest thing for me, was bringing the train back after the Weymouth portion had run in, especially in the dark, loaded with passengers and having very little experience in gauging the speed of the train. Being eight coaches as well, by the time it reached the platform it was gathering speed and the driver relied on the signal to some degree, but it was still up to you to attach the train to the Weymouth portion as gently as possible to the train that was in the platform already with people getting on and off. Most shunters were older than me. Younger members of shunting staff took on the job after electrification, when steam finished. These shunt movements came to an end the following year, 1967, when electrification came into full service.

I experienced some awful mishaps working as a Shunter. The wire that operated the ground signal used to lay at ground level and on two occasions I tripped over it. The first time, the bloody oil lamp went one way and I went another, but luckily it remained alight so I was able to pick up the stinking lamp and carry on as if nothing had happened, and run like hell to catch the train up. Another nasty experience I shall never forget, was when a local train from Brockenhurst ran in. Normal working was for it to be divided, but I hadn't been informed of the change and so I got under from the other side and not the platform side, so no one knew I was there. I was struggling to get the brake pipes apart. Being unable to, the train started to move off. With only a split- second decision as to what to do, I thought, 'shall I lie down?', but there was the risk of being struck on the head by a steam pipe. Really, I thought that it was the end of me as I dived out in between the wheels. How I got out I shall never know. My railway years to come as a Shunter had an element of danger, perhaps that's why I took the job – far more interesting than my previous role as a Porter.

Another experience I had was after dividing a London train. I had put the vacuum pipe on and the brake was created, and in so doing a train will always move back unless the brake handle is partly on; on this occasion, it couldn't have been and the train came back to me. Luckily, I had seen what was happening and ducked down before the train coupled up again. Some years later, it did happen to a Shunter in the carriage sidings. On this occasion it was between an engine and a coach. It was never known whether this was an accident or whether he just wanted to end his life?

After my own experiences, I was more aware of the changes of the job, and by the end of 1966, the station was re-signalled with electric light signalling. I played an important part in this changeover of the movement of wagons when the new layout was being established. I received a letter of thanks from the top management which I still have and treasure today.

BRITISH RAIL: SOUTHERN REGION
Date: 16th December 1966
PERSONAL
Our Ref: T6/5012 E
TO: Shunter Brettell, Bournemouth Stn

FROM: Divisional Manager
South Western Division, Wimbledon

Dear Mr. Brettell

Bournemouth Electrification Alteration Co
Station Layout at Bournemouth Central

I am writing to thank you for the important part you played during the period of the above work. I appreciate the difficulties involved and the fact that the weather was not almost of the best, but due to your efforts, the work was accomplished with the minimum of upset to our passengers.

Thank you for a job well done.
May I take this opportunity to wish you a Happy Christmas.

Yours Faithfully,
For F.P.B. Taylor
DIVISIONAL MANAGER
G. R. CHRIMES
DIVISIONAL MOVEMENTS MANAGER

Me and 1250 Train

1967

By early 1967, the third rail had been laid and electricity was running through electric trains which were able to draw power from the new rail for running in purposes. By April 1967, the very first of the electric trains were starting to run. At the time stock was short; the official date for the completed electric services was 10th July 1967. In April, when the new trains were running, I did three afternoons as Acting Foreman, as it was known then, on the upside of Bournemouth station. This job entailed being in charge of the upside and making sure the trains left on time. On one of the afternoons I was covering the turn, the train called the Bournemouth Belle ran in. This train used to run twice a day, leaving London at 12:30 and then arriving in Bournemouth at 2:10, terminating there. Then the train ran to the carriage siding for watering and cleaning purposes, ready for the return service at 4:40. To travel on this train you had to have a supplementary ticket, which was about £2 extra. Mainly Jews, so I understood, travelled on this train and it was almost always full, coming from London and going back to London too. The Belle had a waiter on every coach to attend to all the needs of the passengers. This train ran for the last time on 9th July 1967.

One particular afternoon I was covering the turn. As Acting Foreman, a job I had never done before, I was in charge of the 'up' platform. A far cry from my early days of farming and milking cows, I thought to myself at just 22 years old. I amazed myself. One of the coaches had brake trouble and I had to decide what to do. There was no examiner on hand - usually they were around but on this occasion he wasn't. The Assistant Station Manager was there but he was no help either. The decision came from Control. Control's job is to advise the Foreman or Inspector what to do in cases of breakdowns to try and avoid delays. On this occasion, I was told to take the coach out of the train station. So, over the address system, I advised the passengers what to do and explained the delay. I then set about getting the coach detached from the fourth coach from the front. Luckily, one of the Porters, as they were known then, had years of railways experience and was a great help to me shunting the train into the bay platform. As the train had no brake, it had to be 'scotched' so that the coach wouldn't run out of the platform. I put the scotches under the wheels. After all these manoeuvres, we got the train together and all set to go 30 minutes late. Just as well there weren't too many trains running - it would have been cancelled if that happened now. It was quite an experience for me, being new to the job, and it seemed that everyone was looking to you as to what to do next. I did do a lot of acting during train announcements that year, and thereafter. I liked doing this very much and have never forgotten the announcements I made. I was once told I spoke like they do on the BBC Radio. I smiled and said thank you.

By June that year, we decided to move from the flat. As always, I was keen to do those things but when it came to it, I wasn't so keen. The idea was to move into a caravan Mother had which had just became vacant. We thought it was a good idea because we were planning on buying a bungalow on the other side of the railway line at Four Marks, which was being built at that time. After moving out I felt sad about it, I guess because we didn't have any proper place to go to. Otherwise I am sure we would have been excited to leave the flat. I guess it must be like this for so many other people in this world no doubt. With all our things at the caravan and realising it wasn't such a good idea, as I hadn't seen the situation first, I found I couldn't work at Bournemouth. Luckily, my wife's father was on his own in a big house. We took the offer up of moving in, and didn't have to pay any rent either, but this saving was cut in petrol by running backwards and forwards to Bournemouth, so as always there was no real financial benefit. Gradually most of our things were bought back from the caravan, in particular the fridge - my father-in-law never had one so that Summer it was a blessing and is still in good working order now at the shop we had years later.

By this time our first born was expected in August, and negotiations were going on between us and the builder for a bungalow. We hoped to buy a three-bedroom place with a big garden, once it was set out that is. The place cost £4,500. I wondered if I could get a mortgage or not on only about £3,500 per year (most of which was made on overtime). In July that year I took my father-in-law up to the place where the 3-bedroom bungalow was to be built, if we got the mortgage. That was all he saw of it as he died in October of 1967, without knowing that we did get the mortgage for the new bungalow. I found myself only being able to get a mortgage for £3,500, which meant we needed to put up the full £1,000 deposit, like everyone else no doubt. I was considerably short of that amount, so it seemed I had to work even longer hours, sometimes twelve hours on a Sunday as well. However, I stuck it out with the hope of moving near the farm and perhaps working it once more.

On 16th August 1967, Mother had come down for the day. It was on a Wednesday, market day, and a hot day as well. I was on a night turn that week, feeling very tired and having trouble with the car. Seeing Mother that day and talking about the prospects of the farm once we moved to Four Marks, it all seemed too good to be true. Unbeknown to me, that night after I had gone to work, Betty my wife was rushed into Fordingbridge Maternity Hospital by my brother-in-law Hugh and his wife Elsie. Hugh, having driven motorbikes all his life and not driven a car for very long, used to drive his car as if he was riding a motorbike. So, she had a rough ride going around corners as if he was on a motorbike! It's a wonder Kevin, as he was to be named, was not born there and then! He was born in the early hours of the morning on 17th August 1967. I discovered the good news in the morning when I got home - no-one seemed to have a phone in those days, so I didn't know what was going on until I got home. The important thing was that everything went well. Visiting hours were very strict - no turning up after visiting times either.

On the Saturday, just after finishing the night turn, the car was completely out use for a few days and it came to a stop just before the roundabout on the Wessex Way. So, I decided to walk a couple of miles back to the nearest 38 bus route which ran to Ringwood, Fordingbridge and Salisbury. I decided to go to my brother-in-law Jim's place near Ibsley. I always got along with Jim and have a good laugh with him. He had a clock and watch repair business at that time and will be always be remembered for his helpfulness. Another long walk too. I was taking a chance for I knew he might have been out, but it was still early, just after 8am. I didn't know anyone else to ask to help get my car back to Bickerley Garage in Ringwood for repair. After getting off the bus, then the long walk down to his place, luckily Jim was up and about and he was surprised to see me, as was I him. I could have done without this breakdown after a long week doing 12 hour night shifts, and still one more to go. I arrived at Jim's place and asked if he didn't mind helping out. He said he didn't mind, getting himself ready.

We set off back to Wessex Way in Bournemouth where I had left my car. By then the traffic was getting heavy. We got back to the car and I tied the rope - luckily, I had one in my car - on to his car and we got going. There was no Spur Road then, or flyover, or hospital as we know it today. It took another hour or so to get back to Ringwood. It seemed at that time that very few people had a telephone, or could afford one, so I wasn't able to let my father-in-law know where I was, or that I'd had a breakdown at just after 6am the morning, with no one to ring up and no mobile phones, and never heard of in those days anyway to my knowledge. I think I had a rest and was not able to go up to Fordingbridge Cottage Maternity Hospital to see my wife and baby boy, Kevin, being our first child.

I was able to borrow a bike from my wife's sister and cycled back to Bournemouth for the last 12-hour night turn of the week. After a hard day, I had a good morning's sleep and was up by lunchtime. Whenever I did this night turn, I used to get bit miserable if I wasn't up by at least 1pm, to have some time to myself before I went back to work for a 6pm start and being on overtime as well. I always wondered how many would want to have gone in to work for a 12 hour shift and a 12 mile cycle each way after a difficult day that I had, but being a reliable person like many others I worked with on British Rail, I remained reliable all my life.

I cycled up to Fordingbridge Cottage Maternity Hospital for the afternoon. The early turn was a 6am start and I had to cycle to Bournemouth Railway Station for the next three days before my Ford Consul car was repaired, as they were waiting for parts. It was well appreciated when I did get it back on the Wednesday. One of the chaps kindly gave me a lift home which saved me a lot of energy that I was getting short of by now, with all the cycling to Bournemouth and Fordingbridge, and usually eight hours of shift work. By the end of the week I had my Ford Consul back on the road and was able to drive to Fordingbridge Cottage Maternity Hospital and collect my wife and son. But Betty had to endure the fact that her father had suffered a slight heart attack from the worry of his older son, Jim, who had a mental breakdown. My wife's other sister came down from the North of England to stay for a week as it all became too much for everyone during that time. Before the week had hardly begun, my wife's sister Doreen went to stay with her other sister just up the road. I didn't really know what the problem was between the family. Jim did get over the breakdown after a couple of months, but still needed treatment for some time after. My father-in-law died on 12th October in 1967. It was sad for us all but no doubt a relief for his having had bronchitis and not being able to breathe properly half of the time. That was an end of another era.

Within a month of that happening, we were able to sign the contract for our first house. Before the signing, it was widely thought by our brothers and sisters that we would never be able to afford a brand new bungalow - neither did we, but we didn't say, just kept everyone guessing… and made it. Even before it was signed and sealed we came very close to turning it down because of a paragraph written in the deeds saying we couldn't have a dog kennel. I didn't want one anyway but didn't see why we should be told what we could and couldn't have - that's all me being awkward. Letters went to and fro between our solicitors and the builder's solicitors. Our solicitor was Mr. Masher, who has acted on our behalf right up to the present day, regarding the shop and the buying of this bungalow as well. He told us it wasn't worth falling out over it, telling us to look ahead. With people moving in and out of house, no one would be any the wiser even if we had a kennel later on, he said. So, we agreed and the purchase went through in 1967. The new bungalow was built in stages right up until 24th June 1968 before it became ready for us. As the months went by before that date, we wondered if we were ever going to move in because very little was being done to the place when we used to go and see how it was going on.

Bungalow at Four Marks

1968

By 24th June 1968, when we were all set to move into our new bungalow, just by chance a job came up in the same grade at Basingstoke. My two weeks holiday came first which gave us time to settle in. All went well with the move to our brand new bungalow on a quarter of an acre of ground to be landscaped by me. I was aged 24 and Betty, my wife, was 22. My first week back at work involved having to drive to Southampton Central to catch the train to Bournemouth. The only turns I could do travelling that distance using my car meant just doing late turns. We did then have our local station called Medstead and Four Marks with a train to Southampton, then on to Bournemouth, but I decided to see it through until the job I applied for came though. Or if I had wanted to do the early turn, it would have meant being at Southampton Central Station by 4.15am and arriving in Bournemouth station about 5.15am for a 6am start. I didn't think it was worth it. This went on for a month, and finally I heard that I had got the job at Basingstoke Station. I was looking forward to being nearer home and not having so far to travel. So, my final week working at Bournemouth Railway Station came to an end and by early August 1968, I took the new job on.

Had I not moved from Ringwood and continued driving to Bournemouth like I was, and not knowing that I would some five years later, I would have been able to travel on the new Spur Road which had just opened. My thoughts were focused instead on starting at a new place and meeting new people. Luckily, I knew most of the train drivers, and they were great people to work with too. A Weymouth train driver who I got on with very well, when we were shunting in Bournemouth Station limits during the steam engine days, didn't mind me sounding off the steam whistle, known as a standard engine, and what a wonderful sound it was too. I almost didn't want to stop, it so reminded me of our early days as youngsters where we lived in Ibsley - when the wind was blowing in the South Westerly direction, we could hear that wonderful steam whistle sound a good three miles away. My brother Brian always knew the time of the train as it approached Ringwood Station.

I had to learn the new layout before I could take the job on, having six weeks to learn in it. With Basingstoke having its own services, all the trains were berthed at night time as they came in. Even so, I passed out for the job six weeks later. It took a while to learn all the times for when the trains had to be in and out of the sidings. They were a long way from the station too, and all the shunting staff had to make sure the trains came out of the sidings on time up to the station. If all went well, ie all the trains were in the sidings by midnight and all the extra work had been carried out, we were able sign off and go home. There was overtime which involved going into clean door handles on both sides of the trains. You used to get a number of coaches to do, say 24, and I used to do them as we took the trains in the sidings in the evenings, which left just a few coaches to do by the early hours of the morning. I finished at 2am instead of 6am and signed off at 6am, although I had gone by 2am, across the tracks with no-one about, to the car park near the sidings, and then on home. Usually it was raining, and it seemed to be wet and cold in that area as well. A good paying turn once you had got started but still didn't make up for the start at that time of day.

As a few weeks went by I found I was missing some of the fun you could have with some of the chaps I used to work with. I found the new chaps very boring to work with. Some of them took the job very seriously, and being a new town as it was, and plenty of jobs going at the new industrial estates, British Rail were never able to keep regular staff, so you were never able to get to know anyone for any length of time, only the older ones who had been there for some time and thought they ran the station. And they did not make it very attractive for anyone to work at the place. On the last occasion I went to work there, on 5th November 1968, I turned up for the 6pm turn in the evening only to be told that the turn was already covered. So, home I went and didn't go back any more after discussing it with my wife.

Mother had previously agreed to get the farm started - I had worked there through the Summer months in the hope of making it happen. Before the month was out, we had 10 Friesian cows, delivered through an agency, which cost £120 each, and everything was ready in the dairy with the cow pen with extra units for milking the new cows. It was back to the wheelbarrow, taking the churns one at a time. Having to have the milk ready by 8.30am meant going down the drive three times, so in time we bought a four-wheel truck to enable me to take the churns in one go. It was a great help having this small four-wheeler truck, but I soon found that wet conditions made the drive awful, with the drive being so rough and a big dip at the bottom which made it even more difficult for me to pull up the other side, so a couple of churns did have to be taken off and put back on. But when the load was lighter, like in all stories, it's the same old thing...make one thing better and you come up against another problem.

By the 5th of December 1968, as anticipated, our second child was born in the morning, a little girl. We called her Karen. Mother looked after Kevin for a few hours while I went to see Betty and our newborn daughter that Friday morning. She was lovely too. I stayed over at the farm for a few days and travelled down to Treelaws Maternity Hospital near Alton in Hampshire. Brian and his wife Julie were also expecting a child, their first. He was staying at Julie's mothers place and didn't get on with his mother in-law too well either. He was waiting for a council house to become available, which it did in 1969. Julie had a little girl as well, in the evening of the 8th December 1968.

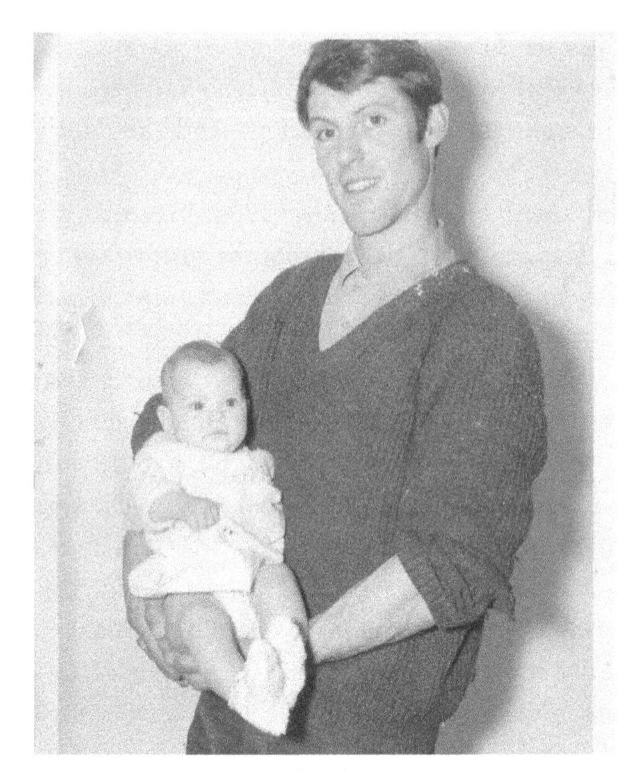

Me and Baby Karen

Sister Christine, Karen and Me

I knew my brother Brian never helped out whenever he come to see Mother. It didn't help making things awkward between us, and he never offered any help at any time. It was a good job that my sister was living at home at that time - I could always rely on her to help me out at almost any time if I was having difficulty with any of the cows. With having a lot extra, it was like a mud bath around the yard, so sometimes I had difficulty in getting them in, and that's where my sister was a good help to me. She also helped when I had difficulty in milking some of them, particularly with a cow I named Kicker who eventually settled down and produced a lot of milk.

By Christmas 1968 Karen was only three weeks old. Her little larynx was working well even though she was only tiny! With the family get-together in our new home for the first time, all went well that Christmas. But there wasn't ever to be another family gathering like it again.

Luckily for me, Mr. Gillies, whom I had got to know when he was working at Alton Railway Station in 1964, also worked in the parcel office at the time when I rejoined British Rail the second time, working in the Goods Yard. I used to travel on the train to his place to see him, so he hadn't forgotten me. I also went to see him and his family to see how they were getting on when I had moved back into the area, in June 1968. When I started at Ringwood, only two months earlier, then left because of the family move to Woodlea Farm in Four Marks, he had a family business breeding rabbits and a potato delivery service around Basingstoke. His intention was to work fulltime from home, which he eventually did. One day gardening came into a conversation we were having. He offered me gardening work from time to time in their garden, which I also did at their house in Ropley, one stop from Medstead and Four Marks Railway Station. Mr. Gilles asked if I would like to work part time, three mornings a week, for 7/6 per hour, which of course, like all good things, meant working some Sunday mornings which I did at times. Like everything else in this life, there always seems to be a drawback of some kind. However, I stuck it out right through the Summer. It did help keep us going, with very little else coming in. However, being the type of person that I am, I was always prepared to take chance where money was concerned.

1969

By January 1969 I was looking forward to the New Year, being a good one regarding the farm, but like all businesses, it always hits financial hard times. With no proper income coming into my household, things soon began to tell when paying bills. Early in 1969 we took in two lodgers which helped our finances at that time a great deal. One of the lodgers, Roy, was in his early days of pop singing and was very good too. We didn't know if he made big time or not, of course he was hoping to. He only stayed about five months altogether, but we still kept in touch a couple of Christmases later. We took on another lodger from Scotland who was quiet. He didn't mind children, just like Roy, but by July, he too had left us for another job in a new area, so that was that. We decided not to take on anymore, which we didn't, from that day to this. In saying that, my sister Christine asked me if she could come and live with us. We were more than happy to have her, and she came to stay the following year. Mother had a habit of saying if you leave here, don't come back. Her favourite was of course her first born, Brian, and it stayed that way, right to the end of her life.

With the farm surroundings looking a lot tidier, and not so much time needed to be spent on it, it left our place looking very untidy. So, I decided to take a loan up through one of these loan companies, which was quite unheard of in those days. Still, I was prepared to take a chance on it, so I could get the place looking good. With £600 to spend, it enabled us to buy 30 new 6x6 fencing panels for both sides of the property. With fifteen panels to put up on each side and 32 holes to dig out, two feet deep, and concrete to fill in the posts and paths to lay, it just about put my back out with all the heavy work I was doing over a short period. Luckily it didn't hurt too much at the time, but by October, I was a cripple with my back. How I ever managed to milk the cows and take the churns down for collection each morning, heavens knows. What did help me was pain-killing tablets that had been prescribed every four hours and trying to rest during the day. However, before that happened, we got the place looking pretty good with all the brand new panels up. It gave our neighbours privacy on both sides as well as ourselves. I put down a wire fence in the middle of the garden and a new gate leading to what became the vegetable garden and fruit bushes. And with 500 rolls of turfs laid in our back garden, the children eventually had a nice lawn to play on. And our lovely Alsatian dog called Greta was lovely too. I painted all the new panels which made them look nice and fresh and I had finally landscaped the garden. A lot more planting came later.

As the saying goes, everything was rosy in the garden. With the view of getting more cows, Mother and I were talking about making a partnership between her and myself, which seemed a much better idea than just working at the farm for Mother and not being paid. But like all these things in life, in theory it sounded a good idea, but in practice I thought it may never work. I lived in hope. I said, if this failed it wouldn't be because of me trying hard to make it work. With the help of my wife Betty, I put up new fences at the farm as well as 4x6 panels along the existing wire fence down by the side of the drive at the front of the property.

On 17th June 1969, Betty passed her driving test in Winchester, after two goes. With being able to drive my Zephyr up and down the long drive over the farm driveway and reversing the car up and down, all the manoeuvering of the car made a big contribution to passing her test no doubt. My sister Christine passed her test a few weeks later in the same year.

Alsation at Woodlea Farm Four Marks

Mr. Gillies had a small potato factory chipping the potatoes into chips and supplying the canteen at Sainsburys in Basingstoke. But first the potatoes had to be peeled and put into the potato peeling machine which took half a hundred weight at a time. All the potatoes had been washed and I collected the peelings to use to make good feed for the cows - they keep up the butter fat and total solids needed to get a steady price for the milk. In those days The Milk Marketing Board paid a lot less for the milk to all farm milk producers, as it was regarded that it wasn't as expensive to feed cattle in Summer as it was in Wintertime. ALL I can say to that is the milk that was delivered to the customer never went down in price either. We as the milk producers, were the losers.

By October 1969, to add to all our other troubles, particularly financially, we noticed that Kevin our son looked as if he had something seriously wrong with him. With a large swelling in his tummy, we took him to the doctor's surgery. That day we were told he would be referred to a specialist, a few days later. After taking him to Winchester Hospital to be seen by the specialist, we were told that he would have to come into hospital for tests for a suspected enlarged spleen. The tests would tell us exactly what the large swelling was, we hoped. We came away from the hospital with more anxiety as to what could be wrong with him.

By this time, we had just taken on some extra cows, making the herd up to 20, with one of the cows giving me so much bother. She may have been used to parlour milking and not a cow pen, so at milking time, and no one to help me out with this, particularly in the morning, it became impossible to milk her. I got in touch with the agent who supplied the cows. After seeing how difficult she was to handle, they agreed to replace her. On the day she was to be taken away, I had to get her into the yard. It was very upsetting to see her go.

I started to realise my Mother wasn't going to do anything more to help me with the farm, after all these years gone by of trying to make it work this time, and with a good herd of milking cows. With all the extra work, and the worry about our son Kevin, it became quite a trial for me at 25 years old. We had got to a crisis point financially, with the extra cost of driving to Southampton Hospital, sometimes twice a day, and not being able to pay my way with our own household bills and the mortgage which didn't help either. Mother's unreliability in making sure that bills were paid on time at the beginning of each month, let alone paying me anything from the little cash flow left from the milk cheque, didn't help either. I began to think that this just couldn't go on much longer. I didn't really think it was Mother's dream, like mine, to have a farm with a herd of dairy cows and be a happy family.

By this time, we had been informed that Kevin had cancer of the kidney and it had to be removed as soon as possible. Then we were told that he had been transferred from Winchester Hospital to Southampton Hospital. This was in the early part of November 1969. With all this being piled on top of our non-existent income and having to go to Southampton every day, really brought pressure on both of us. However, our prime concern was to see him each day, whatever the cost, before the operation. It was all that mattered to us at the time. The few days before the operation, we spent time at Southampton Children's Hospital wondering if he would survive the operation or survive after it. I remember the day before he had the operation, we stayed with him all day, most days. After being told it was a 50-50 chance, it was a very sad time not knowing which way it could go. It was made worse each time we had to leave, because he did not want us to go and leave him. Being an emotional person that I am made it even worse for me too. On this particular day, I recall Kevin looking out of the window at the beautiful blue sky. It was so blue. An aircraft was flying above and with his little finger he pointed it out to me. He just kept saying look, look, as children of two do. It nearly brought tears to my eyes, thinking whether he would survive the operation, and would he be with us this time tomorrow?

During this time, we were able to take Karen to my wife's sister's place in Ringwood. The situation must have been affecting her as it did us, crying so much she was just too much to cope with at that particular time. And we knew her Auntie would calm her. With all the running about to and fro between the hospitals and staying there most of the time, it had become a fulltime job in itself. It made it hard going looking after the animals and everything else that went with them. Well the next day came with some dread, worrying about how the operation may go for our two year old son we loved. We received a phone call from the hospital later that day to tell us that the operation had been a success. That was a great relief to hear for us both at that time. We thanked them very much for all they had done for our little boy Kevin. We went to Southampton Children's Hospital in the afternoon to see how he was, and the surgeon told us what they had found. We were surprised to hear that his kidney had been removed, along with the cancer growth which we understood to have weighed over 1lb after its removal.

We could see him at a distance. He looked to be asleep, but we couldn't bring ourselves to go and wake him up, fearing he may be upset after what he had gone through in the last 24 hours, so soon after the operation. We still couldn't help but feel that he may not have survived after the operation. Thank heavens he did.

Back at the farm I was beginning to think I had taken on too much but felt I could overcome it by taking a job that only required me to work in the mornings. As things began to get worse and worse money-wise, by the Christmas of 1969, I felt I had to do something pretty soon to save ourselves, let alone the farm which I could feel slowly slipping away from me. By this time things had got so bad with no income at all, and the only help we were getting was Mother giving us some groceries. Before any decision was made as to what to do about the farm, we wanted to get Kevin home for Christmas as he had made good progress. This also saved us a lot of expense travelling to Southampton every day. He had to have radio therapy to kill off any possible new cancer cells that might start to grow. This was quite traumatic in itself, having to take him to the Children's Hospital and get him to stay on the couch and lie still while the laser beams were directed at the place of possible cancer cells. On two occasions the visits were wasted. He was sedated in the hope of getting him to stay still while the laser beam was applied, and each time he was upset when we had to take him back to the Children's Hospital only to be left again.

On another occasion I left Betty in the Hospital as she became too upset to leave him, so I drove back to Four Marks where the cows were at Woodlea Farm, to milk them. By this time, it was mid-afternoon. The traffic was heavy coming out of Southampton and the thought of driving all the way back after milking the cows, which took me something like two hours do, was another worry to contend with. Like everything else, I did stick it out, no matter what the cost. I drove back to Southampton only to go through the traumatic event of leaving him and Betty being upset again and Kevin crying, wanting to come home with us. The next day we went back again to the hospital and saw the surgeon, as he had already turned down our request to take him home soon after he had the operation, only on the grounds that they would be able to keep a better eye on him. But with being unable to give him the treatment he had to have, and the upset of leaving him each time, he could see what it was doing to him and us, and agreed that we could take him home, but we would have to bring him in daily for the treatment, which we agreed. By this time the Cancer Research unit got to hear of our plight, and helped us out with some petrol money, which was gratefully received at that time.

Betty drove my car and went to Southampton on her own to see him, as we couldn't bring him home for a couple more days, and on another occasion Betty and Mother visited him. This did give me a chance to get a little more straight over at the farm. Two days later, we were able to bring him home and what a joyful day that was too. It seemed so strange after all, as it seemed such a long time since he was at home. As our garden backed on to the through railway line from Alton via Winchester and Southampton, Kevin loved to watch the trains go by and wave his little hand at anyone on the train. Often people did wave back. Next day we went to Southampton for his therapy to give it another try this time, with the promise from his mother that he would be going home once he had the radio therapy. He just settled down with his little car and rabbit and it was over in a minute or so. This radio therapy was in its infancy stages, so a little too much of the stuff would result in his being very sick or losing his hair. It turned out that it made him very sick. Even though he had not received the therapy until a few days before Christmas, on Christmas day he was very sick, and it was very worrying. It wasn't the happiest of Christmases that I want to remember; thinking he was so much better, then becoming so rough over Christmas - we were feeling pretty low again. A day or so after he recovered, and after telling the doctor at the hospital how sick he had been, I think they must have cut the dose down and he wasn't so bad after the next therapy. We were very thankful to all the nursing staff who helped him to get better.

1970

By New Year 1970, our financial position was getting really bad at home and at the farm. I decided to take a Milkman's delivery job, advertised in the Hampshire Chronicle, which was based on Winnall Trading Estate outside Winchester. But first I decided the only way to raise some cash to enable us to pay for cattle feed was to sell some cows. So with Mother's agreement, I sold two of the cows that we had bought when we started, who weren't giving very much milk. They weren't too big a loss, but I would have preferred to have kept them if I could. This got over the problem of paying for the tonne or two of hay, straw and cattle cake.

My next step was to get Mother to agree to help pay for the hay and straw. She had already agreed with me on a £10 per week, based on morning milking only, so I could take a job with a reliable income, and keep a hand in the farm. By this time, I had applied for the Milkman's job and got it. With a 6am start, at the beginning it was impossible to even think of milking the cows first, as Mother had suggested that I should. So the proposition was turned down. It was supposed to be a partnership but it was no use. All I asked for her to play her part was to pay a share of £10 per week, as she was unable to milk the cows herself or to pay me the amount of £20 that we had agreed to when I left British Rail in Basingstoke in early November 1968. At the time it meant no more shift work for me. I had talked it over with Betty my wife and she was more than happy as I was. We felt it was a new beginning for me to be self-employed again, and to have more time with my children, and my lovely dog Greta. I was never keen on my wife taking on a full-time job, part-time maybe, despite our present financial situation. I felt it was better to rely on one income, whatever the situation. I just liked her to be home for the children. She was very good at making garments with the brand-new electric knitting machine I bought her, and was very good at hand-knitting as well. She made lots of knitted garments, clever in her design, and sold them for a good price.

But the position became impossible for me to continue any longer. My Mother had this awful favouritism for my older brother Brian. For the time being Brian, who no doubt helped to undermine everything I did, had to help with milking the cows instead of me. I guess looking back I should never have given it a thought that I had any hope in hell's chance of ever getting a farm of our own. And with Mother's past history, and having no real knowledge about farming or running one even, I should have known it was never going to be realised. I learned the next day from my loyal sister Christine that our family friend had taken on the job of milking the cows and was paid £20 a week. I was glad for the cows' sake, as Brain had NO real knowledge of milking cows with milking machines, and he, like my other brother didn't have any love for animals, as I did, and still do.

On 19th January 1970, I decided farming was at an end for me, permanently. I climbed up to the top of the railway bank and looked across to the farm and I counted the years; for me it must have been close to 15 up to the time that I had worked hard to achieve what I thought was within my, or our, grasp, including Christine my sister. As soon as we were able to work out some sort of understanding with the overall money situation, being very little of it in our early days, I realised our main priority was getting enough food to eat. I felt very sad while I was standing on the bank, knowing there was no possibility of owning a farm big enough to support us all, and knowing it was the last time I milked the cows. I came away not telling anyone or Mother. There was nothing more to be said. I wouldn't be back even though I only lived over the other side of the Medstead and Four Marks Railway Line. Nevertheless, I felt very proud of my achievement, only being 24 years old in buying this brand new three-bedroom bungalow for ourselves and a lovely big garden as well which I made good for us and our lovely children to play in. Backing on to the railway line, it was a novelty when we moved into the bungalow on the 24th June 1968. Whenever we heard a train coming along, we would run to the back bedroom and wave at it and whoever was on it. We usually got a wave back too. I could still hear the cows mooing at milking times.

On the 20th January 1970, I began having a second go at milk delivery, driving to Winchester every day. I remember the first morning being very cold; when faced with unfamiliar surroundings it tends to put one on edge, and not knowing what to do and having to be told everything, tended to make me feel cold even if it wasn't. However, the round I had been put on wasn't the round I had to learn. My first week was just to get some idea of the work involved, collecting daily milk cheques and cash. I found it a long day setting out just after 5am and not getting back to the depot until 2pm. But the chap I was with the first week was very helpful and we got on quite well. He didn't like getting back too early, being aware that if you finished early, perhaps too early in the firm's eyes, you would end up with another road put onto your round as I experienced later on. So that's why he never rushed around to finish early. Even by the end of the week, I had got to know the round enough to warrant us to finish a little earlier, but he still dragged the time out. By the end of the week it began to get boring, not being able to get on and finish in good time. However, by Friday I had my first wage packet for months. At that time basic pay was £13 plus £2 bonus for selling extra milk, and with working on your day off and Sunday, I took home about £23 as I didn't have to pay any tax for three months. Despite the extra money, I found myself in real difficulties a few months later.

The following week, having two weeks to learn it, I felt I had learned the round on my own. I had to try hard and take it in as quickly as I could, because they were always short of relief staff and I had already been informed by the first chap I was learning the round with, that once you had some idea of what to do, you would have to jog along on your own. And that's what did happen to me, not on the third week but the *second* week. You would have to just follow the book and hope you got it right. Setting out from the depot at Winnall Estate, on through Winchester itself through what is now a shopping precinct, with the round starting at Romsey Hill, the first call was the Council offices and then on to Winchester Jail. In those days you could just drive in and leave one crate of milk, being 20 pints. Then on to the police quarters and the prison quarters. There seemed so much to take in, being so many places to have to deliver to and being January, usually cold or wet, and the electric milk float I had for my round having no doors on it. Luckily for me, the re-organisation which took place in the May of that year, 1970, was a blessing, as the rounds were far too big and that applied to others as well. The rounds were then slimmed down, and if I rightly remember, three new rounds were created. It meant having about 200 pints less to have to deliver each day. Not having to deliver to the police and prison quarters, and a couple of other roads, made the job a lot better and at the time, nice to do. First, I still had to learn the round; it took me about four months and once I had learned it, I didn't need to look at the book anymore. As always with rounds, at every changeover there were always debts left on the book which incurred a lot of extra work. Something like £40 or £50 had to be carried each week on the book until it had been cleared by Head Office based in Portsmouth.

Setting out just after 5am in the morning, there used to be a very good programme transmitted from the BBC World Service. It helped the journey along, especially during the very dark mornings, and being 14 miles from Four Marks where I lived to the depot at Winnall Estate near Winchester, meant I could listen to all of it. It finished at 5.30 am which was when I usually arrived at the depot. The wonderful opening music played, called *Theme One*, was a great piece of music to listen to.

While I was settling down in my new job, and just beginning to like it, on the home front we still needed to make regular trips to

Southampton Hospital for check-ups on how Kevin was progressing and for the radiation treatment. As time went on and Kevin no longer needed the radiation treatment, he was transferred from Southampton Hospital to Basingstoke Hospital. It was thought at that time he may need check-ups for the next 10 years, but August 1980 was to be the last time he went for his final check-up, when he was clear of all cancer. It was another great day to be told that he wouldn't need any more check-ups. We thanked the hospital staff for all the good work they do in helping people like us.

By Easter, I was really getting on well with the milk round, no longer having to look at the book to see how many pints of milk each customer wanted at each place. The milk was 11d (pence) per pint and went up to a shilling a pint in April. A lot of the CO-OP customers paid with a milk plastic cheque put out each day which made it a lot easier for all us roundsmen by the end of the week as there wasn't so much cash to collect, and therefore less callbacks on Saturday afternoons, as expected by the management. By then I began to make friends with several people that I still know today.

With 1,000 pints to deliver or thereabouts, shortly to be reduced, each day and weekends, the round was taking about 8 hours to do. This was the big round as it was before the rounds were re-organised. Keeping hard at it, finishing between 1 and 2pm, it was a relief each time I finished, only to be done all over again the next morning. However, it did feel good, the fact that I had conquered the job. The biggest help to oneself is remembering numbers - this is the time when you find out how good you are, and I clearly was with dates and times which have always been interesting to me. I used to think how good it was by 10am, with only two or three hours to do, and often think back to the shift work I used to do only a couple of years before, and not having to turn out at 2pm like I used to do all those years ago... All good things for many never seem to last.

With the number of roads being taken off my round by May that year, it became a pleasure to do the job. With no more calls around the police quarters, the prison quarters and a couple of other roads, it made the round a lot easier. I had one customer I won't forget in the prison quarters. They were a good pair, meaning husband and wife. They must have been the most difficult people I had come across for paying their milk bill. They had already run up the bill before I came on the scene, only paying £1 or so every week and being told at the office to carry on delivering and keep calling back whenever I could. No help from them. I felt I had enough of them making a lot of work for me, having to call back later in the day and still not getting any money from them, despite leaving an account for the amount owing. They never answered the door when I came back. The CO-OP Dairies never did get their money, I learned later, and they lost quite a lot. Still that's what happens when no notice is taken of the person who is doing the job and knows firsthand. I make a detailed point about this because the Co-operative Wholesale Society (CWS) were very money conscious, and always keeping on to their staff about making sure the customer paid each week. That's how it was. There were even harder times ahead.

Tramping up Romsey Hill from Winchester City in an electric milk float built in 1948, with 800 pints of milk on board, was very pleasant to drive. It was very quiet and much better than driving a diesel vehicle from time to time when the milk float was in for service. It was quite a steep hill too, with no-one about through Winchester as I delivered the milk. As I went on to near the top of Romsey Hill, calling in at the Ambulance Station, having made friends with them, I was assured of a cup of tea every morning and a chat was something to look forward to in the early part of the morning; one group of people I shall always remember for their kindness. Setting off from the Ambulance Station, I usually arrived at the top end of Stanmore Lane at about 6am. And being the Spring, the beautiful hills in the background were always breathtaking to me, every day. I found it a real pleasure to be up here at this time of the morning. Sometimes you could hear the sound of the occasional train in the distance, looking down in the valley from the top of Stanmore lane, near Winchester.

Alsations, Kevin and Car

On 13th June 1970 we went to North Wales for a week with our friends Janice and Kevin. Janice, who was a lifelong friend of my wife's, didn't live very far from us when we were at Four Marks. We were all interested in visiting the area, which was new to us, at the time. It was good to be away from everything else that goes with everyday life. Just us lot setting out with two vehicles. Our friend Kevin drove his mini car and I drove my Zephyr, with Betty and our two children and our lovely Alsatian dog Greta. We followed Kevin at 40mph which made it a long journey, arriving in Rhyll, North Wales, in the late afternoon. The next day we all ventured out to the seafront with our two children, Kevin and Karen, and Greta our dog. We had a good time touring. The General Election was on that week and it would have been the first time I could have voted, but being on holiday and apart from having this week off, I had only had one day off since January. Well as we all know, the election was on the 17th June in 1970. Ted Heath became Prime Minister and three years later took us in to the EEC as it was known then, and later known as the EU. It seemed to make the trip more exciting and was a nice hot sunny week to remember, despite not having very much cash to spare, like most, I guess.

At home after a good week's rest, I was more able to face another week's work. Not knowing it at that time, I found myself working right the way through until Christmas Day; you had to deliver milk to a couple of roads in order to get paid for that day. Working from the June until February without a day off, I found myself becoming a nervous wreck, and had to take time off. Not so much from the work side, but the financial burden of having no wages from the farm and being completely let down by my Mother. What money I had, had gone, and to aggravate the situation, money borrowed to finance the landscaping to our property the previous year didn't help. At the time, bills were piling up again and I couldn't get any more bank support, already having an overdraft of over £200. It might just as well have been a million, because that's what it seemed like, or how I was made to feel. The Assistant Manager was very helpful and understanding, but of course he was guided by what the Manager said. By the late summer of 1970, I found myself being threatened with bailiffs if I didn't pay the two outstanding payments of £36. With all this going on, I was getting solicitors letters from Mother's solicitor, pressing me for £1,000 for my share of the cows that I didn't have. With the worry of all the other things going on and that on top, it made my life, or perhaps I should say our lives, very depressing. I found a very good solicitor to fight the case for me concerning the cows over at the farm. Of course, I didn't know at the time that it would take three years before it was settled. I didn't have to pay anything to the farm as it was recognised that I had lost everything concerning the farm anyway.

Back to the time when it seemed that I was in the line of fire in all directions. Our financial position had met crisis point. We were being advised to sell the property by the Bank Manager at Lloyds, in order to repay the debts, and buy something less expensive. Not knowing which way to turn, after being told what I should do, we were both very upset to have to sell the bungalow and didn't want it to happen this way. The following day, we went to Martin and Stratford, the agent that we had brought the place through, feeling very emotional at this time, having the two little ones with us. They always seemed to pick awkward times to start crying; it seemed for no reason just at that moment but perhaps they were reflecting their feelings in a funny sort of a way, for us. The bungalow was placed in the agent's hands, to our regret.

The following day I went to work as usual and didn't say anything to anyone. I felt I wanted to tell someone what had happened or was about to. Being our first place, and a new one at that, it felt as if I had been carrying a heavy weight on me that day. We started the dreadful trek of looking through the papers at properties, and as usual you can never find anything as good, let alone anything like what we had. The following day I saw the builder, Mr. Offered, who I had got to know quite well, and asked if he needed an extra hand, part-time. As he was still building bungalows down the road, he said he would take me on as long as there was work to do. I felt there had to be a way of finding extra money to enable me to pay the extra money needed to repay the loans. The next day, I set off on my milk deliveries as usual. I had quite a task on my hands - to ring up Mr. Jenkins, the Lloyds Bank Manager, and convince him that I could pay the extra money needed, as I had taken on an extra job and would be working four hours more per day, part-time. I made sure I had plenty of sixpenny pieces to put into the phone box.

I felt I had to win this one, come what may. I felt I couldn't give up the place without a fight. I got through to Mr. Jenkins, feeling very nervous, but very firm in what I wanted. It took some considerable explaining and in the last resort *begging* for the money I needed at that particular moment, which was to pay the two outstanding payments of £36, but after some considerable humming and ha-ing, he agreed. The two payments were paid that day and in so doing, I got the money lenders off my hands for a while. In those days there were no laws to protect people from harassment, and if there were, we didn't know about them. At least the company in most cases would listen if anyone had problems, but in our case, they didn't want to know any of the problems we were experiencing, and that was our main problem. But having got over that moment in time, I now had to find £20 per week just to pay the bank until the account was cleared, which took a few months, with stringent terms that I was prepared to meet under the circumstances.

With only £23 or £24 take home pay it wasn't easy going, but with determination, I was going to get myself out of financial difficulties. It was the first year of the clocks not being put back by one hour, which was a God send, in a manner of speaking. It gave me the extra daylight needed to enable me to work up until 6pm in the evening some days, with extra daylight. This work only lasted a couple of months. However, it did get me out of difficulties at that particular bad time. Being seen up and down the road by the people, it wasn't long before other work followed, which was irregular, but it did help to keep my finances going though that Winter of 1970. The cost of running the car to Winchester every day was £3 per week which seemed a lot at the time.

It's strange really, how attitudes have changed over money over the years. If anyone was having difficulties in finding a few hundred today, it wouldn't be so frowned upon as it did seem to me at that time. As always, it depends on one's circumstances and how and why it happens to us all. After the financial problem had settled down, and I was paying funds regularly into the bank, I seemed set in my mind that I wouldn't ever get involved in any other financial matters again. Especially after speaking to the Assistant Bank Manager, as I had already described earlier, who had an understanding concerning my money problems. He said, "Chris, you will never make it in business, you are just not hard enough." Hearing this made me feel it was really the end for me in respect of ever having a business of my own of some kind in the future. However, I had been told a lot of things in my short lifetime of 26 years. I also remember being told a few years earlier by teachers that I would never get a job if I couldn't read and write. Remembering these things of the past I guess helped me not to think of what seemed to be a failure.

Toward the end of 1970, everything seemed to be going quite smoothly. I was looking forward to Christmas, being my first Christmas on a round. I had heard from the other roundsmen about Christmas boxes, thinking how helpful it would be for me. I didn't have long to wait. Christmas was upon me and soon over like it is every year. Receiving over £50 in Christmas boxes enabled me to stock our freezer with meat which helped us through the early part of 1971. Boxing Day 1962 was the last time it had snowed on that day, until now. What a struggle to get around, up and down the hills in the Winchester area. Chains were put on the wheels of the electric milk float, which did help at the time.

1971

The weather did improve, thank goodness, by the New Year of 1971. New Year, new hopes like most, but as time goes by, we soon find what we hope for invariably never happens the way we want it to. In some cases, no matter what we do to make things come about, it just doesn't happen. But I received a nice letter late in 1970 from the Head Office telling me how well I had done, regarding keeping debt very low compared to how it was when I took the round a few months ago. The book had carried over £30 a week, and I had got it down to only £5 or £6 each week. I was very pleased to hear that the CO-OP Management had recognized my good efforts in doing this round. I liked the job very much. I got along with many customers I had come to like and they must have liked me as I was often assured a nice cup of tea. One tends to put ones all into it, but in a very short time things soon began to change. I was also taking on any gardening work that came my way, whenever gardening came into a conversation.

By early February I had a couple of the former roads put back on my round. It had been less than a year - I thought it was too good to be true. As usual, no consultation, you just come back off your round and when paying in the milk cheques, you were just handed pages out of the roundsman book. If you asked, "why the change in the rounds?", you were just told that some changes were needed on a couple of rounds. Perhaps it was to take on some of the extra customers that had changed over from Unigate, or some made-up rubbish from the Foreman, terrified of the Area Manager. You couldn't get any sense out of him. He didn't want any bother, just a quiet life. I guess that the Management had put extra roads on several rounds to try and slow us down so we couldn't get back so early. Still, I was told this right from the beginning, that you could expect more put onto you if you got around too fast. That's life, no different for anyone, I guess. Being an extremist, I went the other way and dragged the deliveries out, getting back late. But I didn't like that either. One foggy morning I noticed the Area Manager's van in the distance. I decided that I didn't like finishing late either, so the very next day I got around really fast, finding the extra delivery only taking me an extra 20 minutes, and getting back to the depot near the old time of 12 noon. It must have given them something to think about no doubt!

After that things settled down again but I didn't feel the same about it. Looking back, good times were had by being able to finish by 12pm, and if it looked like being a nice day, I would phone home and suggest to Betty to catch the train from Four Marks Station to Winchester, where I would meet my family after I finished work. We either went to Ringwood for the day, visiting, or stayed in Winchester, or whatever. Like all good things, the Alton-Winchester line closed two years later. However, we made good use of it while I worked at Winchester. Other than that, things had settled down regarding Kevin's health. He had improved and it was comforting to know he was going on alright. By this time Kevin was able to go to nursery school which he seemed to like.

I also began to look at different jobs. One was in the prison service, but I didn't fancy working inside, so I didn't go any further with it. I looked at other jobs, but none ever came up to my expectations, so as the saying goes, if you don't know what to do, don't do anything. At Soke Hill Garage where I bought my weekly fuel, the owner sold out to a firm called Impact, a London based firm. It was 'new broom, sweep clean' with new staff and everything changed around just to make thinks look good; as always trying to make an impression on everybody. I got to know the Manager while I continued to buy my petrol there, despite not being keen on the change, and it became useful later.

As the clocks didn't have to be wound on that year, I enjoyed the Spring and light mornings. It was nice to be out in the mornings but it wasn't to last. By early June I had another two long roads put on the round, and once again without consultation, just like four months previous. I found the area to be the scruffiest place that I had ever seen for Winchester. I think it must have been for some of the dropouts. I was shown where the places were for a couple of mornings. Most of them were too idle to put the bottles out each morning, and when they did, some of the bottles were never washed and awful to pick up being Summertime. So, I told them all, as and when I saw them, that they would have to put the bottles out at the front and not round the back of the house as they had been left in the past. I was giving them the same as they gave me – a rough time. It only lasted a month before it came to an end.

Before giving the job up, I came up with an idea that would perhaps bring in a few pounds. I started selling potatoes and eggs, which went quite well. I had about 300 leaflets printed and bought 1,000 plastic bags to put the potatoes in. I found a place which sold the bags I wanted in Winchester. It set me back a few pounds but I was soon able to get the money back on the bags. I remember telling the Assistant Manager at Lloyds Bank about my new enterprise. As the Manger, Mr. Jenkins, came out of his office, the Assistant Manager told Mr. Jenkins with enthusiasm about my idea, but he didn't seem quite so enthusiastic. Perhaps to be expected, but I felt quite embarrassed for the Assistant Manager who was trying to make me feel that it was a good idea. Anyway, it wasn't to last, just like so many things I have tried. It was quite funny when delivering the milk, putting the leaflets under the bottles, getting a round going within a round.

Once I had got a potato and egg supplier, I was set to go once the orders were received. I would get all the bags of potatoes ready in the afternoon and load them up with the eggs in the boot of the Zephyr and deliver most daily. Being new potatoes, there was great demand for them until the Winter when orders dropped off. Before that, I had to smuggle the eggs and potatoes onto the milk float without anyone knowing. Quite surprisingly enough to my knowledge, I don't think anyone knew what I was doing. If they had found out that I was delivering eggs and potatoes while delivering the milk, I might have ended up getting the sack, knowing them to lack enterprise themselves.

I even took a chance on delivering milk every other day, after I had persuaded some of the customers that it was a good idea and would save me a lot of running up and down these long grass banks which divided the houses from the road. You certainly wouldn't find so much ground not used today on new estates, that's for sure. The CWS were so rigid about the milk being delivered daily, as they were in stiff competition with Unigate Dairies. There was talk, from Unigate at the time, of no milk being delivered on Sundays, but it didn't come about until 1984, some 14 years later. By the end of 1971, my little enterprise had come to an end. I didn't think it was worth carrying on with, with only a few wanting small amounts, so that was that. After I wished I had kept it going. Still, we all say the same thing after the event.

By June 1971, I was determined to keep up the momentum regarding not taking the milk round to the back doors, side doors and God knows whatever else these people could think up to make the job as awkward as could be. It seemed to me I hadn't experienced anywhere else on the round the previous year which was so bad. Gradually, I persuaded just about all the customers to leave the bottles on the front doorstep where I delivered the milk. I had one who had a box on the wall. It was awkward for anyone who delivered the milk there. They were retired with nothing to do but moan about me or anyone else who didn't do things just right for them no doubt. Anyway, this is how I saw them. Having milk cheques, they would insist on putting the cheques inside the box under the bottles. First you had to go through a side gate, always bolted, and sometimes they wanted one, then they might want two pints… so sometimes if there was no cheque, they got no milk.

I mentioned it to them, requesting them to please leave the milk cheques somewhere else other than putting them at the bottom of the box. But this was declined, with them saying that if they put the cheques anywhere else, they could get lost. I explained that most people left the cheques on the doorstep, with well over 200 homes leaving the cheques daily. It still made no difference to him and his wife. I should add, they were both there looking out for me each day, just to see what I had to say no doubt, so I decided that as it was too much trouble for them to try and help me, I wasn't going to put myself out for them. So I would go through the gate as normal, but instead of putting the milk into the box on the wall as requested by them, I just left it by the side of the wall, opened the box and took out the cheques and empty bottles. That really got them going the next day when I arrived: they were both waiting for me and I was in no mood to give in to them either, no matter what happened. On this occasion, the battle came to an end. With all the naggling going on between us, one of the pints of milk slipped out of my hand straight onto the concrete where it smashed. They must have seen red, seeing me perhaps as no more than a youngster. Anyway, I was just as annoyed as they were. The couple phoned Head Office at Portsmouth, no doubt complaining all they could, which led to me being suspended. It must have given the Area Manager great pleasure in ringing me up when I got home and telling me to report to the Head Office at 11am the next day, the next day being a Wednesday as I remember. By the tone of the Area Manager's voice, you were to feel that it must have been all my fault. Funny how human nature tends to jump to the wrong conclusions before we even find out as to what really happened.

My other and last encounter with one of the customers that I was delivering the milk to, was an ex-Railman. He had worked at Winchester Station as a Foreman. We had got on quite well after I had mentioned that I had worked for British Rail at Bournemouth, so we had something in common, particularly regarding the earlier days. He used to tell me how hard things were when he was my age. Anyway, when I decided that I wasn't going to take his pint of milk round to the side door, that did it. To get him to leave the empty bottles and milk cheque or cheques, whichever the case might be, I would go around to the side door to pick up the cheque or cheques and empty bottles and leave the milk on the front door. That really got him going. Quite a big chap as well if I remember rightly. However, it didn't matter what he said, the milk was going to the front door and not the side door as he insisted.

With another set to about it, he said he could see no reason why I couldn't bring the milk round to the side door. I retorted by saying, "You were telling me about the hard days when you were my age?" and that "I could see no reason why I should have to take one pint of milk round to the side door." As he was retired I then said: "You have all day to come and pick it up off the step." He didn't take kindly to that either. I never did take the milk round to the side door. Even so, I had to go around to the side to pick up the cheques. Neither of us won the battle. It was just the same in 1964 when delivering milk over at Avon Castle - some of them wouldn't let the vehicle up their drive so you would have to walk up the drive with one or two pints sometimes, and if they needed extra milk, it was back up again. Just as well I didn't take the round over there, that's all I can say! I don't know if it has changed today or not. One would hope common sense would prevail. The odd thing that I found difficult to understand was that they were all council houses and all were ordinary working people, apart from the drop outs, so I couldn't see why some of them were so awkward.

Setting out one June day, nice and sunny as I remember, we decided to make a day of it and go to Southsea. First, I called in at Head Office for the 11am meeting. Unbeknown to me, my representative from the General and Transport Union, who lived down Stanmore Lane where I delivered the milk daily, was there. He must have asked the Relief Milkman who I was, or the relief chap might have told him. The odd thing was he used to have a Unigate delivery and only came out and bought pint off me because I was a lot earlier than his Milkman. He must have told them exactly what he thought in that office and told them how reliable I was, working almost every day of the week, which was true. As I saw it at the time, being in the office, from what the chap was saying, he recognized that I was reliable and so on. He thought I must have gone a little haywire since I last saw him as a few months before he was thanking me for getting the round debts down to a low figure.

To explain why all this had come about, I told him I had extra roads put onto the round, with little consultation. He replied he did not know about that, of course, and he went on to say that the Rep had spoken for me on my behalf, explaining the incident. He agreed that it was unfortunate what had happened, and said: "Could you just put the milk in the box to keep them happy?" The Area Manager was chipping in, saying: "It's what other roundsmen have to do to keep customers happy!" I thought to myself, "Yes, I will go along with what you say and be like you: say one thing and do something else." And that's what I decided after agreeing with them, to carry on quietly and give notice on the Friday of that week. I felt if I couldn't win, they wouldn't win either. They would have to find someone else to put the milk in these stupid boxes round the back and side door. Before giving notice, I made sure I had another job to go to but as always, I seemed to take a job less well paid than the last one. However, working out the cost of getting to Winchester every day and the wear and tear on the car, I thought that I would be no worse off. And having my gardening jobs, I would be able to make my money up to £20 per week again, which meant working almost every Sunday. As always with these kinds of jobs, as the saying went, if you wanted a Sunday off, just say, but I never did.

It so happened that the manager of the Soke Hill Garage was looking for a Petrol Attendant, and after agreeing to the hours and rate, it was shift work once again. However, as I didn't have to get up so early every morning, and it was only a mile from home, and I could use my bicycle, I thought that this would probably be better. Giving notice came as a surprise to them in the office. After telling most of the people I had got to know quite well that it was my last week, some were quite sorry that I was leaving and others recognised that the firm didn't deserve anyone any good. That did help as I was sad about leaving the place, however I kept in touch with quite a few, but as always people pass on or move and you never hear from them again as to what happened to them.

I decided not to work on my last Saturday but as always, I woke up early. I went for a long walk taking the two children. Having got them dressed they were quite keen to come with me at 7am in the morning, as they weren't used to me being home in the mornings. Karen was only 3 years old and Kevin was 4. So, we set off on this long walk, Greta coming with us. By the time we came back I was really tired and so were the two children. It wasn't such a good idea as I remember. I started a new job with no holiday either. It made that year seem all work, and working only late turn by request, as I had a lot of gardening work to do. Looking back, I had no social life, just work and I was still haunted by financial problems from the year before. Like most people, that seemed the only way forward for me.

By the August, I decided to sell the car, which I did for £80 as I thought it would need too much money spent on it. But I found in a short time I made a mistake in selling it and had no money to buy another one at that time. It just meant we didn't hardly go anywhere. My sister, who was living with us at the time, did take us out and about, but since her car was a Hillman Imp, it was just too small for us all and wasn't very enjoyable for any long distance.

It wasn't surprising our costs doubled the way it did after Decimilisation in 1971. With all the pence added to just about every item that was sold at the garage, we were led to believe by the Manager that putting a few pence on the items would keep the till straight, and if there was any money over by the end of the week, it would be shared out between the staff (there were four of us), but that didn't last long. We were soon told that we were just breaking even. We were also informed that if there were any shortages, we would have to pay for it out of our wages at the end of each week. Being fair to the Manager, that directive came from the Head Office, but luckily for me that never did happen — just as well as I wasn't getting that much in the first place. So instead of sharing any tips or extras that came our way from customers, we decided to keep it, instead of paying it in and getting nothing at the end of each week. As we saw it, the customer said: "keep the change", so it was ours to keep. It might have only been a £1 per week, but at least it was used to pay for our electricity. Southern Electric was very helpful and suggested we have a 5p Meter to pay our bills at the time, which we gladly agreed to. It worked out at £1 per week. That was one thing less to come out of my fantastic wage!

The other good thing that came out of this job was that green shield stamps were given away with petrol, and the best thing was, if any customer didn't want them, we could have them ourselves. Soon I was getting a book-full per day and two books on Sundays. That was the only good thing about working on Sundays. With petrol costing £1.42 per four gallons, and the firm giving out quadruple stamps, I managed to save something like 50 books of stamps by the time my employment had come to an end in November. The book being worth about £1 each, it enabled us to do all our Christmas shopping for most of the children's toys and other things. Once I filled a Rolls Royce 33 gallons to top up a 40-gallon tank, and he didn't want the green shield stamps either! Just before my employment came to an end, there were checks on the amount of stamps that were given out according to the amount of fuel, so while the checks were taking place, we didn't get any stamps. It wasn't recognized by the Management that if the customer didn't want the stamps, the firm should benefit and not the staff. It was suggested by Management that we could have over-estimated the amount of stamps given out each time and ended up with far too many stamps being given away to friends or to people we knew at the firm's expense. That wasn't true either. By early November, this job suddenly came to an abrupt end. Having worked on the Sunday, by the Monday late afternoon I was told that they were cutting back on staff and I would no longer be needed, and that our one week's pay would be sent on to me or if I could call in for it, in a week's time. I didn't see why I couldn't have been paid on the Monday, especially as I had worked on the Sunday. My other workmate had worked on Sunday as well. There was no union we could have joined either and we didn't expect to be treated the way we were as we were all reliable staff.

Having sold the car in July, I was left without any transport and no money to buy another, just like so many other times that seemed to happen to me. The only thing I did have was the secondhand bicycle which I bought for £5. I bought a new one later for £25. One week passed and I found that I had no wages to come from the garage - I was told that I wasn't entitled to any and had no-one to help in this kind of situation, as it often is the case for so many people. Betty, my wife, was most upset by it all. Same again I said, for it didn't matter how good you were, I found myself being let down again. We just had to struggle through the week until my unemployment benefit came through. I thought to myself, ONE day, I may find a way that I could run a business of my own and support myself, my wife and my wonderful children. But in doing so I would only let myself down if my willingness was taken advantage of by others. By chance, a friend of a friend knew I did garden work and other jobs. I was offered a job helping to renovate a small bungalow overlooking the Mid-Hants Railways Line. This helped me through another difficult time until another job came along.

By early December 1971, I was looking hard for a regular job, although at the time I was thinking of going self-employed again, even though Winter wasn't the best time of year to go self-employed. By chance I was on Winchester Railway Station, waiting for our local train to Medstead and Four Marks, when I saw the Relief Station Manager who I had got on well with when I worked at Bournemouth Railway Station. I asked him if there were any jobs going at Alton Station and he replied that there were. He said they would be glad to take someone on with the shunting experience I had, as there was some dividing to do and the occasional shunt from platform to platform. After talking it over with my wife, I decided to take the job as a Railman, formally known as a Porter. So, for the third time, after passing their medical, surprisingly I was back with British Rail.

Work consisted of making sure all doors were closed on departure of all trains when the Southampton train came in every hour. Being a single line from Winchester Junction, the train had to have a key which ensured that the Signalman had made communication to the next signal box which was Alton. The key would be placed into a locking device and pressing the plunger on a bell would ring at the Alton box. The Signalman would acknowledge it by pressing the plunger which rang a bell back, which in turn released the key and gave the all clear for that section of the line. Once the key had been placed into the locking device, it couldn't be taken out until the Signalman released the lock from the other end, which is all part of safe travel on the railway. The key would be exchanged at Winchester Junction, and the Signalman would hand it straight to the Driver through the signal box window. Then, in this case knowing the procedure, I would meet the train on arrival. But as I was always late, I had to run up the stairs and down the other side to collect the key, which was carried in what would look like a purse with a handle. I would commence down the platform, over the crossing to the signal box and hand the purse over to the Signalman and he would go through the usual procedure. Being there only a few weeks, I soon got back into the job. It was a 6am start, cycling from Four Marks to Alton and being able to take the train back home. The station was only a small one and didn't have enough staff to cover the turns, so that meant doing overtime at the end of early turn, which meant staying on until 3.30pm every day except Sunday. Being that small, there wasn't enough to do, in my view, of interesting work. Where so many things had been cut out, there was less to do; no fires to light, all gas. Six years previously it was all gas lighting, having to go around with a pole to put the gas lights out. Another job cut out. As time went on, the job began to get me down, having to stay there every day until 3.30pm. Of course, I could have said that I didn't want to work every day, but that would have upset the routine.

Although I got on okay with the chaps I worked with, they were all in their 60s and would never do anything out of routine, which made it very difficult for me too. Of course wages being what they were, low - I suppose the rate then being £17.20 per week - one needed to do overtime, but my feelings were not every day, and that was one of the problems working at a small station, covering the rest of the turn. Worse still was weekends. Being a commuter station, there was even less travelling in the early part of the day. It became so boring. The chap I worked with was a lot older than me, not that that makes any difference because I have worked with chaps the same age and you would think they were 60 in their movements. However, that didn't change the situation. He used to be so miserable and didn't speak for hours at a time. If I spoke my mind, he wouldn't speak for days. At least I knew where I was. He came around when he was ready. I wasn't going to crack that easy. I had been through too many hard times before. I went there to work. My Mother was surprisingly similar to us at home, so I tried not to let it bother me, too much.

The only good thing was that I got on well with most Guards and Drivers and used to like playing pranks on them. As it was a turnover service, the train would stay in the station for half an hour, so it enabled me to chat and have a cup of tea with them too. To get to our staff room, we had to go through the alleyway and it had a heavy thick door at the entrance. I would let the Driver and Guard walk through and slam the door behind them as hard as I could, making such a good bang, and of course making them jump as they weren't expecting it or anyone else around at the time. Nevertheless, they saw the funny side of what I did. Better than being miserable. The ones that perhaps weren't so cheerful, I didn't play around with. I also had my radio playing almost all the time in the staffroom. Some good music played on the BBC too. The other thing I used to like doing was crashing the old two-wheel carts. Heavy iron, well-made they were. We used to burn the station rubbish in the disused Goods Yard and once over at the yard, I would run like hell and let the old cart go, tipping over and everything on it. That's how I felt after being there towards the end of the day and it felt as if I had been there for days, it was so boring.

1972

The only good thing about doing shift work was it gave me time to work on my garden at home. By this time, May 1972, other gardening jobs came along for 50 pence an hour, but it would have been no good trying to run a business on 50 pence an hour, as it had crossed my mind then to get into garden maintenance. I just wasn't sure how to, so like most of us, I played safe and stayed in a job which in some cases I hated doing. Before the railway job came along, we talked about putting the bungalow up for sale. Six months later we did without any success in selling, and had we sold it then, we were planning to live in North Wales and possibly buy a small holding, or to live in Herefordshire. Not knowing the area too well, it might have been a bad idea, who knows? It didn't come about. The other reason for the move was to get the children settled for they were about to start school. Kevin had already started at a local school and all was well for him which I was glad about. It would have been harder for them later perhaps!

With the threat of the Mid-Hants line closure that year, there wasn't a lot to look forward to, with even less to do if it came about. I used to get quite involved in writing to our local MP and to anyone else that might have been interested in saving the line from closure. Clearly he was just like the rest of them. I had some support from the Booking Clerk who helped to cheer the place up and was good to have intelligent conversation with about things in general. With house prices going through the roof, our bungalow was on the market for

£16,500, but as I said, we didn't sell. It wasn't meant to be go to North Wales or anywhere else at that time.

In May 1972 I had a week's holiday and for me it relieved the stress of the Alton-Winchester line's possible closure. We went up to London first, across London Kings Cross, and changed for the local train to Boston, Lincolnshire, and stayed with Janice and Kevin for the week. Not ever having been, it gave us a chance to visit this part of the country and the town of Boston to see how different things were. I also tidied-up their garden for them too, while we were there. Our friend Kevin took us about the Lincolnshire countryside, which was very nice too. That week soon went. As always, we tended to think what to do for the future, but I always felt whatever I did I seemed to make life harder for myself by more work. The closure becoming nearer, I felt I would have to make a choice: to stay on at the railway or make the move and try and get a job back at Bournemouth where I preferred to work if I had no other choice. I tried working at Farnham on overtime but didn't fancy working there full-time either.

By this time, a job was advertised at Alton Station for a leading Railman, but no-one applied for the job because of the Parcel Office. However, I knew if I got the job, I would receive £2 extra per week on the basic rate. I got the job and the extra rate of £2 a week. I would just carry on covering the Railman's position - some prospects being one of those all your life! After three months, if you haven't taken up the position, you were automatically paid the rate, which I did receive, and never ever did the Parcel Office job. I was after getting my former job back at Bournemouth Station as I could see the line was going to close sooner or later. The rate for Senior Railman here was £24 per week, as opposed to my rate of £21. By November 1972, there were rail strikes galore, and no trains on Sundays. Some of those times it really got me down — a place can only be cleaned up once. My sympathy was with the Drivers as they couldn't do any overtime, like so many other grades on the railway could, but at the same time I didn't agree with some of their tactics. By the end of 1972 it became clear that the battle to save the Watercress Line, as it was known as, was lost. By this time, I had three good gardening jobs going working for Dr Wheeler.

Dr Wheeler was a Doctor of Science and wasn't hard up, which helped me along. He was a great help to me, at that time. I also did the garage and one other place. Kevin used to come with me in those early days and play while I worked in the garden — to think 13 years later he helps me a great deal in my gardening business and knows a great deal in his own way!

Christmas 1972 saw us with our new colour TV. My brother and sister-in-law, Hugh and Elsie, stayed with us that Christmas and were as keen to see everything in colour as we were. I ordered the new colour set to arrive just before Christmas and not telling my wife that we were going to have one was a total surprise to her. When it did arrive, her words were "but we didn't order a set?" thinking that they had called at the wrong place. After all we were hard up the year before. The set cost £300 and the size of the screen was 26 inches.

1973

In January 1973 I had been working one full year for British Rail, and by this time the date for closure for the Alton-Winchester line had been set for 3rd February 1973. All it meant for me was seeing less of the local people that I had got to know through being at the station, and it made the job less interesting. The line should have been electrified, after all it was a through line. The powers that be don't care about what the people want, only what *they* want and that was to close it down as if it never existed, never mind the history of how the line came about and was built. However, all the opposition against the closure didn't make any difference. Before I looked around, the final day had arrived. It was a Sunday and hundreds of train spotters with their pac-a-macs were travelling on the extra coaches provided. I can only describe the pac-a-macs people as the kind that wore macs and packs on their backs and took lots photographs of almost anything that moved. They asked people like me a lot of questions about railways. For them it was an eventful day, for me a very sad one. At the same time, once the closure had taken place, the Mid-Hants Preservation Society was quickly formed, and many people joined it and subscribed £1 or whatever. That's what I did in the hope that the line would be re-opened in the not too distant future. But trains didn't return to Alton Station from Mid-Hants until May 1985, some 12 years later. Many of us had left the area by then, for good perhaps. After the big event, which is what it seemed like on the 3rd February 1973, it left me even more in the wilderness as to what my next move should be. British Rail wasted no time in having the rail line taken up. Heaven knows why they needed to take the line up, other than to make as sure as one possibly could, that the line would never reopen again. By 1977, Alresford Station reopened, which as a family we visited to celebrate the reopening. The rail lines were re-laid in the station.

The weeks turned into months and by May that year, we decided to put the bungalow up for sale once again and see what became of it. Luckily, seeing the line was going to close, I had bought a 1962 Zephyr for £200 from a garage at the top of the road. The car did me a good turn for four years before being scrapped at a value of only £13.40. Two weeks after putting the place on the market, this time for £15,000, we had a buyer with a firm offer of £14.800 which we accepted. But, no sooner I had said yes, in my indecisive way, looking at the garden and how nice I had got it and full of vegetables at the time, made me feel very unsure, I guess. Probably it's the same for a lot of people who decide to move. But for us the difficulty had only just begun in trying to find a place as good as we had, which is always the same unless you are able to afford a place for twice the amount, which we didn't have. So, like most, we got fed up with looking at properties and by July, we very nearly called it off as we were unable to find anything as good as we had. It's always peculiar how things do turn out if it is meant to be that way. In our case it must have been, because no sooner we had decided to call if off, we found a place similar to ours, being modern, and we liked it straight away. So as in most cases of buying properties, the wheels were set in motion. This time, there was a mortgage shortage and our own building society wasn't able to lend the money needed for this house, an extra £6,000 in total. But I was borrowing more than I needed, partly to write-off a loan of £1,800 from the previous year.

Despite my previous financial difficulties, I wasn't going to let to many things stop me from getting what I wanted. I had intended to buy a new Ford as a new model had just been released and at that time there was a sales promotion going on. In the hope of selling the new models, they lent out the car for two days for a free trial, which I gladly took up. I traipsed all the way to Winchester, left my car there and drove the new one back and we had a day out in it. I felt on top of the world for those two days, having had an older car and not being used to it. The following week I did the same thing again. I went to Southampton, Hendy Lennox show rooms, leaving my car there for two days, and drove the new one home. I took the children out in the morning to Southampton first before returning home and taking the new car to work. But two days later I was back to the older car again.

Fortunately, we found we could raise the £6,000 we needed, leaving enough for a new car. The new loan came through the Leeds Building Society, linked to an insurance policy which ran out after two years. A week later I set out to Winchester to the garage where I first loaned the Granada, and ordered one just like the one I had driven. I was there a good two hours or more, going through the extras I could have put in the car. But that wasn't to be - the car would have arrived before the sale of the house had gone through. I tried to raise £1,200 for the new car from the bank, but as the sale wasn't definite, that was that: no new car until we had the cash. But when we did eventually have the cash, we couldn't get the car because of difficulties at the factory.

The 17th August 1973 was the day for the move from 20 Winston Rise, Four Marks near Alton, Hants. Being our very first place and as it was a brand new bungalow, it was very hard for me to leave it, as it always is for me. Wherever I am for a certain amount of time, I always get attached, especially as I had laid the garden the way I wanted it. However, once you make a decision and the place is sold, you have to go through with it. Leaving by midday, after saying goodbye to those we had got friendly with after five years, quite a time, was sad for me. Down at Ringwood, we moved into the new place. I wished I was somewhere else - that's how I felt that day. It was also Kevin's Birthday and he was 6 years old. On the Sunday, I had arranged to work a late turn at Alton Station for the last time. Travelling up, I had to go by our place which was on the way, thinking 'no more picking the children up and taking them with me to work'. After working the turn for the last time, I said goodbye to Sam, but the other chap Ben no doubt was glad to see me go and I kept out of his way as much as possible. On the way home I went by our old place again and felt better for doing that.

Monday arrived, the day of my return to Bournemouth Station, after five years away and not having too many new acquaintances to make it a little easier to get started. I just had to wait for a Shunting position to come along but didn't have to wait too long. Even so, some said it was fixed. Knowing the job as I did, it was to the Management's advantage to have someone that knew the job. By the October of 1973, I took the Shunting position over and was no longer floating about the station covering different turns. The going rate for the job at that time was £24.95, with £3.95 extra on my basic. At this time, October 1973, a chap joined British Rail called Kevin Higgins, and he became a good friend over the next seven years I worked at Bournemouth. In some jobs, if two people think the same almost at the same time, it can make a job so much easier, instead of so many other peoples' attitude: 'that's not my job'.

Me and Shunting Colleague

By this time, the threat of petrol rationing had started to make it difficult to get petrol to travel to Bournemouth every day. Luckily it didn't happen, it just cost more – 60 pence per gallon at that time. The country was beginning to look poor towards the end of 1973, especially with all strikes that were to take place, including the railway. But before that, there were thousands and thousands of club parcels that used to come in by the trainload and almost all the Shunting staff had to work 12 hours, 2pm to 2am, or 2.30pm to 2.30am, to help out. For me, I used to like doing the turn that no one else liked doing, and that was 4pm to midnight, but while all this parcel work was going on, I would work from 4pm till 4am. Every parcel had to be sorted and reloaded for the Weymouth line or for the Bournemouth area. Really it was a waste of time having to sort through these parcels, when they should have been properly loaded at the depots, instead of having to work through the night sorting them out just to do the same thing the next day. No wonder Parcel Trains were done away with forever in 1982 and with big losses.

1974

1973 and '74 was the time when all the rail stoppages were going on, including no trains on Sundays at all for eight weeks. This was due to the train drivers' union ASLEF being in dispute with British Rail Management's over pay. Plus, the current political situation didn't help at that time. Government versus Trade Unions didn't help the railways at all. As for us National Union of Rail Members, we weren't in dispute, so we were able to work our normal Sunday rosta, until the end of the eight-week Sunday and weekdays of stoppages. BR could no longer stand the losses, so they booked everyone off on the last two Sundays of the stoppages. There were no trains, but due to the General Election being called in early February of 1974, the weekday and Sunday strikes were called off (of course depending on the outcome of the election). Most of us I guess hoped for a Labour Government, if only to get away from the continuous battles that had gone on for the past two years or so.

As we all know, it all had to be faced again within 10 years, but this time I feel, people had had enough of Trade Unions trying to run peoples' lives in some cases, as well as the country. The Labour party won the election on the 28th February 1974, with a few days delay over constitutional matters. By early March, the Labour Party became the Government once more and everything looked rosy, so most of us thought. At that time, I was quite a believer in social justice, so it was suggested by the chaps that I worked with that I should put myself up as a candidate as a staff representative, to represent members of staff over any grievances and try to get Management to move obstacles from beside the trucks, and anything else that we could fall over in the dark. The only good thing as I saw it which came out of the 1974 election, was the Health and Safety law which was a great help to us at that time, because there were so many obstacles left lying about and trying to get by was impossible before the Act came about. This was one thing that the Trade Unions had fought for, and was in many cases a good thing, but in a lot of cases, the chaps didn't want to be safety conscious. I always felt that too much emphasis was put on pay by the Unions, and not enough on time off, particularly in our type of work being shift work. I know a lot of people always wanted to work, and that included me, but when you had to have your proper rest days off, you soon adjusted to the financial situation. Like everything else, we tend not to stick to any one thing, like myself. We had to have our rest days off, partly due to being fully staffed, but after getting used to a lower amount of income, I found myself getting by and feeling a lot better for it. By 1976, the financial position had improved. Staff in our grades took other positions, so that left a position to be filled only by overtime and being paid time-and-a-half. Most of us worked these days, sometimes I think, just to see how much we could earn.

The introduction of shift allowance by the previous Conservative Government, to take effect on the 1st January 1974, with 60 pence per day, was a little more encouraging. But like everything else for me, it didn't change things in respect of doing late and night turns which I grew to hate. Luckily for me, a chap called Mick Standing came around from the West Sidings and took up one of the Shunting positions after a short while. I found it costly getting into Bournemouth all the way from Ringwood, and knowing that I didn't like night turns when they came around every seven weeks too soon, he indicated that he would do all the night turns for me and others who wanted to exchange his turn. In my case it turned out to be an early turn, 6am to 2pm, for the horrible night turns. This lasted for me right from 1975 to the time I finally left BR in July 1980.

In January we were expecting our third child any time and I made sure that I would have a week off work, by arrangement. We also planned to have this child at home with a midwife attending the birth. On the morning of 2nd January 1974, Betty went into labour. I called the midwife as arranged. I know there was a big sigh of relief from Betty and I when the midwife arrived. At the time our other two children, Kevin and Karen, were with me downstairs in the lounge. I was a little anguished as I had mixed feelings as to whether I would prefer a boy or a girl. I thought to myself, you often speak with other couples that are wishing for a boy or a girl and often it didn't work out for them and I thought it would be the same for me. We could hear lots of sounds coming from the bedroom and our third child was born. When the midwife came downstairs to tell me we had a baby girl, I was overjoyed with the news. I felt I had not only been blessed with Kevin and Karen, but now our new born who we called Nicola.

In June 1974 my holidays arrived and we booked a holiday through Hoseasons for a two week boating holiday on the Grand Union Canal in Wales; the only holiday that I spent £200 on and it turned out to be a disaster, for us not being able to get through the locks and having 3 small children. It was awful. The only thing that made us laugh was when we went under a disused bridge. There were two small lads waiting for us to go under the bridge and as we did, they tipped a can of water on top of us and then they ran off. At that time I let Kevin steer the boat so the poor little chap got the lot over him. It was funny the way they did it. We thought they were onlookers but soon found they weren't. After going up and down this piece of canal, and at one point nearly falling in myself, trying to get the boat off a mud flat, we had had enough after four days. So, we gave the key up and went home on the Wednesday. That was the end of boating holidays for us. I had a go at getting my money back as I had felt that we weren't shown how to operate the locks, taking my complaint to my MP and taking the trouble to go and speak to him myself about it, but he was unsympathetic toward my case. He had to say something I suppose. This went on right into 1975. It was discussed on Jimmy Young's programme. I was sent the script after it had been talked about on his holiday advice programme at the time. I was talking to the

Further Education tutor about it. She suggested I take legal action, but I decided to write to the *Daily Mirror* instead. As always, advice is easily given. After trying what was suggested, I didn`t getting anywhere with it, so after months of haggling, I let the matter rest.

1975

In 1975 with the Labour Government in control and Mr. Wilson as PM, it still didn't bring any better industrial relations to the railway. By June 1975, there was once again a threatened rail strike by the NUR, which included me. Again, all this for another pay rise. Mr. Foot was the Employment Minister then, full of sympathy as always before an election, but after an election they forget — not that I was for a strike. In lots of cases there is no need for them, only hot-headed Union leaders getting carried away. Or in some cases during those times, Unions got so involved with Government, they forgot about their members and as we all know, never even asked what their members wanted. That all changed 10 years later. By mid-June 1975, the threatened strike was called off and our pay went up to £39.50, but once again, fewer people were using the trains because of the possible stoppages and Higher Wages Bill. Within weeks, savings had to be made. With better pay after the settlement, all the positions were filled. That meant our rest days off were hard to get used to, when we had been used to working most of them, but once we started having those days off, we were glad of the day off in the week, especially being the Summer months.

By August 1975 I decided to buy a Honda 70, costing £204 on the road. Never having driven a motorbike before, I wasn't looking forward to the trip to Bournemouth each day. However, the cost was a quarter of the price of the car to get to work, 60 pence per week. Once I had got used to it, I went on for the next five years and hardly used the car, not having a very good car to start with. By November, the car ended up as scrap at Wards Scrap Yard near the Ringwood Railway Station that was. Neither of them are there now. I only received £13.33 pence for it - it was like starting all over again, in some ways worse than starting again, having had a car. It was months before I bought another one.

Towards the end of 1975, inflation was very high and as always, our heating bill increased to beyond what we could afford so I decided to try and have our gas boiler taken out, even though it was the in-thing to have gas boilers put *in*, and not taken out. This would make way for a coal fire, but in my case a wood open fire to save us from hefty gas bills. Being on shift work, I had half a day to cut all the wood we needed (no point until the boiler was taken out). Two firms messed us about instead of saying they didn't want the job. They must have thought we were mad, wanting it done. By this time, I had run out of cash, so I gave up on the idea for the time being. By February 1977 we came across an advert for putting in solid fuel boilers. On the 23rd of February 1977, the boiler was taken out, costing £100, and we sold the gas boiler for £40 a few days later. We only bought four bags of coal to start with and it wasn't long before the wood soon poured in. Once I had a car again, by March 1977, I was able to go looking for wood more easily, something you never see these days. I had chaps giving me wood when they no longer needed it. By then I was working more and more at the Goods Yard, and after asking if I could clear any old wood away that was laying around the yard, there was plenty to keep the fire and the heating going, and it only needed the effort to collect the wood and saw it up. Another colleague and friend who I worked with helped me cut some of the wood up into small pieces, so that I could carry a small bag of wood on the back of my motorbike.

The Zephyr 4 I had bought for £120 seemed a good buy, but as always buying privately, no return on the amount involved, and the car was ten years old — I was the seventh owner by then. It wasn't until 1977 that I could afford to get it put on the road. What a relief knowing that I wouldn't have to face another Winter going to work on my motorbike. I don't know how I got through the previous Winter with the occasional snowy days and very windy days which nearly blew me off the road if I wasn't on my guard. Just luck, I guess, that I didn't come off my motorbike in such awful weather conditions.

1976

In March 1976 I was offered to go on an Industrial Relations course but had to travel to Beckenham, Kent. I was keen to travel and no-one else was interested in going; too far for some of them. Catching the 6.20am from Bournemouth to London for the five days, I arrived back in Bournemouth at 7.20pm in the evening. It was good just to say I did it if nothing else, and to get the extra pay, as we weren't getting very much overtime then. By the time I returned to my normal working, the Management had new proposals to cut out two positions. I would be one of the first to agree to making jobs more efficient, but as always, the people who suggest these cutbacks were not affected financially.

We found ourselves having to disagree with the set of proposals and hoped we could delay it for some considerable time. As always, the chaps brought it on themselves in not carrying out the job properly, but the real annoying thing about it all was we would all have to do a lot more in effect, for less pay. I couldn't agree to the proposals with good support from the staff, so we were able to put off the change until 18th January 1980 before it became effective. Several left the job before it came into effect, others took different positions within the railway and many went for different reasons after I left in July 1980. The only reason it was delayed was because the Goods Yard was on the cards to be closed. This took time to organise, regarding staff and transferring it all to Poole Goods Yard, which was only to close itself a few months later. So that was a waste of time for the staff, transferring only to be made redundant a few months later. All were given other jobs later, we understood.

A colleague Kevin and myself mainly worked the Goods Yard between us for the next two years, from 1977 until it closed on 1st June 1979, as they didn't want to fill the positions for obvious reasons. We worked with one other Shunter, Dennis, who knew the Goods Yard workings inside out. We used to start at 6.45am in the morning by letting the shunting engine into the yard before the arrival of the goods train from Eastleigh, and let the train run into the yard. Sometimes it would have 40 or 50 wagons. Once the train was in, we shut the points up and let the train set back, then detached the wagons, mainly coal and some empty wagons for reloading, for Bournemouth. Once our wagons had been detached, the front half would run onto Poole. It's rather ironic because in 1975 I was going to start the gardening business, but due to the very hot summer, and very little grass needing cutting in 1975, and 1976 was the same, I gave the idea up for the time being. I was there five years in all and had a good time up at the Goods Yard, if you can call it that, sawing up wood in my spare time, and putting a bag of wood on the back of the motorbike every day. The loads I brought home already cut into pieces ready for burning kept us going, and Dennis was keen. He used to help me saw the wood up too, and with the help of some of the train drivers, we used to load a wagon from the bottom of the yard and bring it up to the top of the yard and cut it all up eventually.

Me Sawing Wood

In March 1976 we had to have our Greta put down as there wasn't any treatment for back legs trouble. It was very upsetting for us all losing her. I decided not to have another one, but Betty thought differently to me and went for a rescue dog called Pip. The children loved him too and enjoyed taking him out for walks with their mother. But Pip seemed to like going off on his own, which was disappointing, and we had to go looking for him, until one day we couldn't find him. In the children's Summer holidays, I went home during the day and would pick them up and bring them to the Yard for the rest of the day to ride on the engine. My son Kevin would come up to the signal box I used to operate, letting the trains in and out of the Yard. I was able to cine film Kevin pulling the signal lever, and the points levers, which he couldn't quite pull, being only nine years old. Watching him struggle with the levers made it all the more interesting to look back on years later. He loved having a go.

With the Yard being run down, we used to get less and less freight coming in, and that in turn gave us more time on our hands sometimes. My colleague Kevin and I used to go for a bike ride around the town or I would go to my brother-in-law's cafe and chat to him for a while and then come back and cut up some more wood. With all the good friendly helpfulness from drivers, and many other chaps we came into contact with, we really wished it wasn't going to close, but just like everything else in this life of course, all good things come to an end, sooner than we expected in this case. Later, Winter 1978 brought heavy snowfall, which some people may remember, when the milk was not getting through from the West Country, so the milk tanks were drafted into Bournemouth Goods Yard. This gave us a lot more to do whilst the Wintery conditions lasted. It made us feel important with all the milk lorries unloading their milk into the milk tanks. We had to have the train ready to leave on time in the evening.

The main part of the freight trains sometimes contained steel of up to 1,000 tons. The trains used to come up from Poole and Hamworthy Goods Yards, to make the three smaller trains into one, and usually it went out from Bournemouth Goods Yard double-headed, coupling the two engines together. We would have it ready for departure for four minutes past 3pm. During that time, with less and less Goods Trains coming in and out of the Yard, Management asked for two volunteers from the shunting staff. I was one of them, my college Dennis was the other. He had many years' experience working in the Goods Yard and was a good work mate to work with. We were to be trained to operate what became a part-time signal box. I regarded it as an achievement to have passed out for this signal box, and I have a photograph of myself at the window operating the signal levers. As foretold in the earlier part of this story, being in farming I never imagined operating a signal box on British Rail.

Me and Signal Box Levers

With the Signalman in, once we got release from the main Bournemouth signal box, I would set up the road, as it was called, and record the time. Once the train had cleared the points, the Signalman put all the levers back, rang back to the main box and told the other Signalman that all levers were back in position. Then it was time to close out and get over the main line, being very careful not to step on the third rail, being electric; with 700 volts running through it, we had to be extra careful when working over it or near it, which I clearly was. After all that, Management would ask if I would cover part of a late turn of 4 hours, usually covering for staff on holiday or no staff. For me being keen for a challenge, I used to double-back and do four hours' overtime for extra money. I would motorcycle the 12 miles back to Bournemouth Station and work another four hours. Usually I could get away before 10pm once the last train had been dealt with. Of course, this meant no home life with my wife and children. I expect most chaps thought I was crackers – I think I did myself sometimes. There were a couple of times I did 6am to 2pm on Saturday and returned that same night at 10pm to 6am – only twice and that was enough! The extra money just wasn't worth it. I saw it as just another challenge. Part of my life has been full of them. When I did regular night turns, the week ended at 6am on Saturday morning. I would often return for the 2pm to 10pm late turn on Sunday, then come back again at 6am on Monday morning. I guess if I hadn't done all this, I wouldn't have been able to have write about my shift workings experiences! The main reason for all the problems with covering the turns of duty, was none other than that the pay was so low, and if all the job vacancies were filled, the pay would have been even lower.

Nearing the end of the Goods Yard's life, I became restless, as early as 1978, not being able to see a future in the job I was doing. It always worked the other way with me: the less I had to do, the more I became down and depressed. One of the things I will most remember, is when the wagons used to be loose-shunted, meaning that the vacuum had been let out of the cylinders. Then they were shunted off from near the top end of the yard, with a shunting engine pushing them fast enough so that they would run down to the end of the yard on their own, with a Shunter waiting to catch them, in this case being me. The Shunter detaching the wagons instructed the driver on the shunting engine to push the wagons at a short distance at speed. We were still handling coal wagons on this occasion. Three trucks of coal came down at speed, each truck of coal weighing 20 tonnes, 60 tonnes in all, and if you didn't slow them in good time, right down, they could end up over the top of the stop block, which did happen sometimes, I understood.

Luckily it didn't happen to me. With only handbrakes to stop them, you had to run beside them and drop the heavy iron break handle - as they were very heavy, they helped to slow the wagons down. Then you had to put the shunting pole under a bar that was provided, and press down hard on the brake handle, as hard as you could, then run to the next one and do the same, and the next. On this occasion it was a great challenge knowing that it consisted of 60 tonnes, just about stopping it with only a bump on the block. Whenever we ran beside these wagons, we just hoped we didn't trip over. Not too many years ago all this had to be done in the hours of darkness with only an oil lamp to see where you were going. It was the same in the station with Parcel Trains that usually came in after midnight and had to be unloaded by the night staff. I helped unloading the parcels as well, after all the parcels had been sorted and placed in the right order ready for delivery. Being the night Shunter, I had the job of rearranging the parcel vans in the right order for off-loading at other stations after returning to their depots.

When night-shunting, my first job was to tell the Driver on the shunting engine what moves had to be made and arrange with the Signalman for the points to be changed when needed. Using an oil lamp to signal to the driver for each move, I used a white light, waving the lamp from side to side. Then I switched to green, if making an attachment, and red to stop. That was my early days of night shunting with an oil lamp. One night I asked why the wagons had to be loose-shunted. The simple reason was there were too many wagons to shunt, and with so many different roads for them to go in and hand points to pull, it would have taken too long to place the wagons individually. These experiences will be remembered for a long time to come.

Most Good Yards closed in the late 1970s. I had had work experiences at Ringwood, Alton and Bournemouth Goods Yards; something I shall always remember, as well as the chaps I worked with and the shunting engine and train Drivers who were great people to know at Bournemouth Railway Station. After the yard had finally closed on 1st June 1979, it was back to the station carrying on our normal duties, and several had left the gang as I mentioned earlier.

With the 1980 Winter over, I thought about taking on garden jobs as a business, which I had been thinking about as far back as May 1975. It became a hot, dry Summer. I thought there wouldn't be any gardening jobs so I didn`t even put the ad in the local paper that I had already written out. I kept it for the following year. In 1976, another Summer loomed upon us all which was even hotter and dryer than 1975. With no rain for months and months, I gave the idea up for the time being.

I received a call from Hucklesbrook Farm and I was asked if I would like to do some part-time tractor driving, bringing in the bales of hay from the fields, and I said yes. I loved the idea of being back on the farm that I had such fond memories of in my earlier years, and of being on one of the most efficient farms I had ever worked on. I enjoyed the Tractor driving experience, pulling a big trailer of hay. At the same time, I helped out in milking their dairy cows. It made me wonder if I could go back to milking the cows was my thinking. But the gardening business was on the horizon and definitely not farming.

1977

In 1977 I was asked by Mr. Budd, our Rosta Clerk, one of the Management team I got on well with at the station, would I like to work in the Goods Yard full-time, as one of the shunting staff was retiring. I said yes with some enthusiasm as my first thoughts were 'no night turn working!' I expect he knew he could rely on me saying yes, which made his job a lot easier, as all turns of duty were meant to be covered. Then, not knowing the outcome of an advertisement that I placed in the local paper, I found myself with a flood of calls all seeming to want their garden to be maintained. At first, I wasn't sure how long it would last, so I did the work in the afternoons after I had done my normal shift and found myself turning all the overtime down at the station. It didn't seem possible to think I was earning £50 or more in a couple of days, when it took all week to earn that on the job I was doing. I started to buy things I'd never been able to afford before, and I think some of the chaps must of thought that I had come into money, especially as I was turning down overtime. Only a few knew what I was doing.

As I was earning a lot more money than I was getting at BR, I decided to give notice to leave. This was after 13 continuous years and only a few months to go before I would have been eligible for sick pay days, which I could never afford to have off like most when feeling rough. Some days, as one might imagine doing shift work, I got bad headaches - one of the drawbacks after working a late turn followed by the early turn and a lot of long hours. It's surprising how mixed the feelings were when it was known that I was leaving. Most of the chaps I knew couldn't imagine me doing anything other than what I was already doing. But as I had experience in doing so many different things over the years, at the age of 36 and always geared up to work hard at anything that I felt was well worth working for, it wasn't too difficult to do. Funny though, if anyone ever left the job, it was always said, "he'll be back" and in some cases this was true. I only hoped it wouldn't be that way for me, that I wouldn't have to go back to BR for another job involving shift work, which I never want to do again. I liked working for British Rail, but there's no family life in shift work.

The hardest part of the garden maintenance business was pricing the work. But that did come with experience. Like most, if I under-priced it, it made some jobs a little harder going but you just had to grin and bear it. Wondering if another job would come along was always at the back of my mind. You tended to do all that was going. Another reason for this was that I never had a lot of money, as there were times I had a job to run my motorbike, let alone pay all the household bills and the family to look after - all the other things that go with running a household. But I struck lucky. One of my first jobs was over at Avon Castle, a job I had priced at £70 - a good start. The work he wanted done I did in about two and a half days, so I was able to save this and not have to pay it straight out as I had other jobs in between. I soon had £100 or so, something I wasn't used to in such a short time. But I knew I had the Winter to get through, so the big test was yet to come, with a big tax bill too. The first to benefit apart from myself, from my change of work, was my children, especially my son Kevin who was 13 years old. He liked to come and help me on Saturdays with my younger daughter, Nicola. Our Alsatian dog Kirsty also loved to come with us. It became a real family gathering at a lot of the places I went. I got along with most people, carrying out gardening and clearance work, which I loved doing and was good at it too. As time went on, Kevin earned a few pounds for himself as well, and so did Nicola.

1980

The other thing that took some getting used to was the amount of cheques received for work done. Again, it needed getting used to, partly because I only paid a few pounds into the bank, but was used to saving a large amount from my weekly pay at BR. My weekly amount was stopped through the Railway Savings Bank and I drew cheques as and when I needed to pay bills. One thing was for sure, you never had to worry about getting overdrawn, as one usually can with ordinary bank accounts. By 25th July 1980, when I left British Rail, I no longer had a weekly amount of £40 coming in, which provided just enough to meet all the bills at the time when my basic pay was only £55 per week. All that changed, being paid daily on most occasions. My priority at first was to buy as much equipment as I thought I needed at the time, and get it all paid for. Like many before me who have started up in business only to find they perhaps have bought the wrong type of machines, I hoped to rectify these mistakes without too much of a loss. But life became wonderful for me, having my children with me as and when they were able to. There was an air of excitement I felt after many years of being in jobs that could never have given me the way of life I have now. Funny, since I had tried self-employed as far back as when I was 16 years old.

As grass cutting season came to an end, I had new, regular customers. I continued clearing the rhododendrons over at Avon Castle for a new house that was to be built onsite once it had been cleared. It's surprising the challenges you are presented with, such as using my new motor chainsaw that I had bought for £225, and quite a heavy one, having never used a motor saw before. I didn't think of getting ear defenders like I should have done. It just wasn't thought of as being important in those days, but I did soon after. I was working on a steep slope, cutting down big tree-like rhododendrons. I'd had previous experience using an electric chain saw as our Mother had bought one in 1961, which was a miracle, after we had given up on selling bags of logs for three shillings and sixpence. My older brother and I delivered the logs using his vehicle within a 12-mile radius. We soon realised the price was too low…another one of Mothers failed schemes. It did make life a lot easier for me in not having to cut all the bags of wood needed to sell, using the double-handled saw, and to keep the Rayburn going and cooking by it too. At that time, you could buy a core of wood from the Forestry Commission, sawn and delivered. It took a lot of skill, strength and determination using one of those saws on your own. I was only 16 years old but soon handled the 21-inch bar chainsaw very well, despite the noise which I didn't care for.

This particular clearing job came to an end by early December 1980. Before that time, we went to Jersey for a 10-day holiday, something else I could never have afforded before, since it cost me £700. As a family we will remember this holiday for a long time to come, especially as we had spent our honeymoon in Jersey 15 years previously in 1965, and it was a bit of a celebration with our three children. It was the children's first flight as well. We travelled on the British Rail ships from Jersey to Guernsey. The sea crossing was a little queasy on our stomachs, and the same coming back, otherwise it was nice to visit Guernsey, again. Seeing the lovely Jersey cows was a treat for me too. It was October, the weather was pretty good and our children had fun on the beach making sandcastles, a bit of a competition between them as to who could make the most. I had my cine camera, bought in 1976 for £36, and did some memorable filming of us all.

One of the greatest things about buying the cine camera was being filmed by my work mate Kevin. I am thankful to him for his professional usage of the camera when filming me carrying out my work. He filmed me joining up the Weymouth portion, being four coaches to the train to London, and detaching engines from the Weymouth portion. I have a good film of me carrying out the detaching of the Engine at speed. I was always full of energy as it shows in the film. I was also lucky to have footage of me running at speed across the track in the station and springing up onto the platform which I always loved to do. I never saw anyone else doing what I did, running across the track and springing up on the platform, in all the years I was doing the job. In 1977, the BBC hired a train for a programme called *Nationwide*, which was the name on the side of the train. I remember watching the BBC film crew filming from the station footbridge, a BBC presenter getting off the train, in fact he did it twice.

Me and 'Nationwide' Train

By Christmas 1980, the clearing job had ended over at Avon Castle. This meant losing £36 per day for the two days that I worked there, but this did include working two half days on Saturday and Sunday mornings. Sometimes I couldn't get out of the habit of working on weekends, particularly Sundays. It took me a good year before I decided not to work on Sundays at all, unless the weather was really against me. Luckily, that's not been too often, or better still very rare.

1981

The Winter in 1981 wasn’t too cold as I remember, but the garden work had dropped off drastically, so I was glad I saved what I did to get me through the worst of the Winter. It could have been a very tricky time if you didn't believe in yourself, as people were telling me that it wasn't a good time to go out on your own with the Recession. That's all we ever heard about. Early 1981, my wife had left her job working in a fabric shop and decided to open a wool shop in the Shopping Centre. She needed £3,000 to get started and I was very much for it, but it wasn't long before I found that I could have done without that to concern myself with some three years later, with my own business finances to worry about.

Advertising on a regular basis started to bring in new business by early June 1981. Despite it being a wet Spring, I seemed to have enough work to seek a young lad to help me and perhaps give him a chance to learn something useful. I took on a lad called Anthony under the Government scheme. I paid him £25 per week and claimed it back at the end of each month. Like all things that seem to be good, I found myself relying on him but then he would start taking days off or wanting time off when I needed him most, or just expecting the next day off with no warning. It soon became pointless in having him, so the same year I took on a chap to work three days a week at £2 per hour. Being a little bit older, he was a great help and could keep up with me. As it was hard going, I decided to take another lad on under the same Government scheme, but that proved to be a waste of time as well. I wondered why they bothered — perhaps they didn't realise gardening work is so hard going. I thought by the end of 1981 that work would drop off as it usually did, like the previous year. So after all the bother and the unreliability, I decided to do the work on my own. Knowing that Kevin, my son, might have difficulties in getting a job himself, I thought I would leave a space if need be for him, although I knew he wasn't too interested in taking on gardening work full-time.

During the previous year, 1980, I had become very interested in astrology and sent off for a life reading which cost me £8. It forecast that within a year or so, I would have a lot of material things, which I feel has come true. My Zephyr was 15 years old and had given me a lot of trouble with the gear lever falling off miles from home and the windscreen wipers dropping off. Imagine driving miles in the rain with only one wiper working on the opposite side! On another occasion, the car caught fire where I had left a blanket under the engine. Luckily, I had some water with me, as there was no one about so early in the morning and was no odds to anyone. However, in its strange way the Zephyr kept going in one form or another. The last lot of problems I remember were when I ran about with no dynamo or fan belt and kept the radiator cap on loose. I had to charge the battery each night until I could get it fixed.

I was still unsure about how long my business might go on for. I had seen the kind of vehicle I wanted - a new one would have cost over £4,000 and that would have been for a one tonne, 500-weight. I think my indecisiveness helped me on this occasion because had I been able to buy it, I would have ended up with too small a vehicle. So with not being too sure about my own business, I felt that if it didn't last for any reason, I would still have a good car and could probably pay for it with a less well paid job if my business had fallen through. So by the 10th August 1981, I had a nice R Reg Granada, setting me back just over £2,000. I had put down £500 with two years to pay off the balance. I felt I had done quite well one year on from starting the business. It had been some 12 years since I had had a decent car. Only a few months earlier, I had also spent a few hundred pounds on a large new tent so we could go camping at weekends.

1982

I felt the hard work of the past year had been worthwhile, but as we all know, it seems easy to get things but keeping them up when the chips are down can be hard. In 1982 I found myself helping Kevin on his paper round every Saturday morning, usually setting out just after 6am; dead keen I must have been. We did this for three years in all until he turned 16 and had to give the round up. Karen took over for only a short time. I only helped her a couple of times as she didn't seem to want any help, and she gave up the round shortly after. I had enough of getting up early every Saturday too, so that was the end of the paper round deliveries in the Brettell family.

Business as always was very quiet during the Winter. As to be expected in any outside work, the weather plays an important part and for this reason I have it quite good as there is no snow in this part of the country, just very cold at times. Nevertheless I never let the cold weather stop me from working when there's a job to be done, if I can help it. This time of year was also a good time for the wool shop as wool always sells best during the Wintertime as one would imagine.

In the Spring I saw a friend of mine, Pat Evans, and his wife. He worked at Bournemouth Station as a Train Announcer for a good many years. I also use to do train announcing during overtime and I liked doing it very much. I didn't think Pat would leave British Rail as he was much keener than I, but with the continued run down in staff, after I left British Rail, there had been no escape for anyone. If the position wasn't needed any longer, that was the end of the job. So that was that. He sold up and bought a place in the Outer Hebrides, Scotland. A good place if you don't want to see anyone I guess, as we all feel sometimes! After saying goodbye to them I thought about an expedition to get to Pat's place up in the Hebrides. For me the Spring and Summer were a good time to take the family camping to Wales at weekends and for the holidays. The trailer I had bought that year was a great help to me on these occasions.

In June 1982 there were a lot of thunderstorms. With a lot to do, as always at this time of year, I rarely gave in to rain. If say, I was cutting a hedge and if it came to rain during the time I was cutting it, even with the thunder and lightning banging and flashing, I just carried on and took my chances and got a bit wet as I wanted to get the hedge finished by a certain time. That's how keen I was to get something done. Of course, I realised afterwards how dangerous it was that I could have been struck by lightning. I said to myself I wouldn't do that again and I didn't.

By late Summer, a brand-new shop became available in the High Street. It was being lined up at a cost of £100 per week which Betty thought would be better for her business. There were more risks to be taken with more money needed to get the place ready, as it was only an empty shell when we first took over in early October 1982. That was on the horizon and my own business needed something new to give it a boost. Again, I needed a lot of cash to enable me to buy what I thought I needed for this. With my old car nearing its MOT and needing a lot of repairs, I thought I would try my luck and see if I could get a new Ford transit truck. I thought a one tonne/500-weight would have been ideal. A representative came out from English's of Fleetsbridge and made me an offer of £700 for my old car, which was 16 years old, an offer one would try not to turn down. The vehicle I wanted to buy was going to cost £5,500, and minus £700 of the £5,500 still left me with too much to borrow. Worse still the payment were too high and there was a risk that business would do no better than if I just carried on with the old car which at least was mine.

I telephoned the Second-hand Sales Department of English's and asked if any trucks were for sale. There were two; a two tonne non-tipper and a two tonne tipper. I tried them both and made the right decision as I went for the tipper, and an offer was made of £200 for my old car. I still needed something like £1,000 for the deposit that I didn't have most of at that time. The vehicle cost £4,500 and even if I could find the deposit needed, it still meant another £125.66 per month to be found for the next three years, so I knew the risks were high, at least that's the way I saw it. With a bank loan already in hand, and other big payments on other things I had going, I became very indecisive as to what I should do. The Sales Manager was very helpful because he understood, I felt, what it's like taking on these kinds of risks. He got the Rep from Ford Finance to phone me, who took details of my financial position at the time, and he said it looked favorable. It was still left as undecided as the overall amount to be repaid was over £5,500. As with so many businesses you see, they look to be doing well on the surface, but underneath they could be doing badly, and I didn't want that to happen to me as the business had only been going for two and a half years. I have found that you're never really taken seriously until a business has been going for some years - that's human nature I think.

Just at the time I was trying to make the decision on whether I should buy the truck or not, a clearing job was in the offing. I thought if I got the job it would cover three monthly payments on the truck. So I had to raise that deposit, made the appointment at the bank and asked for £700. Even if they agreed to lend me the £700, it was still risky having another commitment on top of the £125.66 per month, plus everything else. I was in two minds about trading in the Granada as it was worth a lot more than the old car, but at the same time if I did, I knew I wouldn't get another car like that one in a hurry for the kind of money that it cost me, so I left that in the background for the moment. Once the bank had agreed to the loan of £700, I immediately went ahead. Of course it would have been much easier to have borrowed the lot from the bank, but having a great deal of experience of banks and their thinking, I didn't want to get too deeply involved with them; as it was I already had a big enough loan going so I thought I would play it safe. The deal looked as though it was going through, when I received a phone call to say that Ford Finance had been in touch with my bank and told them that they thought I had enough to pay for without taking any more on. They said the most I should borrow was £2,000, something like £2,000 short, so I thought that was goodbye to ever owning one of those vehicles. I kept this to myself and only mentioned it to my family when I had achieved what I had hoped for in buying this particular vehicle.

The Sales Manager knew I was very disappointed. He said he would call me back which he did later. With being unable to raise even a small amount of cash, he solved the problem by raising the price of the old car. The agreement was that if I failed to keep the payments up, I would lose the vehicle. On this basis, I agreed after some thinking about the risk involved. On the 15th September 1982, I took delivery of the truck, something I always wanted and probably the finest thing I have ever bought that produces such a good return (to be realised later). We were all pleased about the outcome of buying this vehicle. The Sales Manager did say something which I do believe. He said that Ford Finance were very flexible to people like myself. As I saw it, they took a small risk and I felt the chance was worth it because having the truck meant I would be able to take on bigger jobs. I didn't know if it would pay off or not at the time. All the same, good job they did take the chance as within less than 3 years, all payments were made in full, on time and two months' earlier than agreed. With many more thousands needed and all the problems I had with Betty`s shop, I think I had had quite enough for one year regarding money.

The following week the clearing job came about. The site had to be cleared of bramble and small trees for a housing development by the side of Wellworthy's. It's just as well, because it was a very wet Autumn and very little gardening was going on at the time, but I carried on regardless. It seemed to rain for most days while I did this clearance work which was finished by late October. Then the shop had to be made ready. After the plasterers had finished, it had to be painted out which I did myself, starting just after 6.30am in the morning, each morning, so as to get some of it done before I started my own work, usually at 8.30 or 9am. All this preparation had to be done by ourselves, ready to be open for business by the 3rd November 1982.

Just to add to my troubles, the mowers were on the verge of chapping out, which one did. I guess some of that was partly my fault through lack of maintenance. However, that didn't help me. At the time I had to get another one quick, so as to keep going. I thought I would raise the cash through an existing finance company, as I already had a loan going with them. Days went by only to be told that they couldn't help me, so I didn't waste any more time looking for finance. I borrowed £100 from one of my children - I had given it to them all a couple of years earlier - and paid her back a few weeks later when the cheque came in for the clearing job I had done. At least it was paid for, but it wasn't a very good one. The mower I wanted cost £236 instead of the £136 I had paid. Still, I thought it would help me at the time.

1983

By the following Summer, 1983, I had bought two new mowers, trading in the mower which wasn't very good, and I also bought a new hedge cutter. The lot came to just over £3,800, paid with interest by a new finance company. I paid it all back in less than a year. It's all a chance, but taking it at the right time is the thing in business. That's how I have found it myself. At the start of 1983, another new year, I looked back at the past year, like most I would imagine, at my past achievements, in particular on the amount of business I was doing. I felt that something new was needed. I had something in mind when purchasing my first truck in September, in 1982, and after buying this I felt I could do more with it than carry two mowers, but I didn't quite know what to go for. I studied the ads in the local paper. There were no ads for rubbish clearance. I thought there might be a lot of people who may wish there was someone who would undertake the clearing out of sheds and garages, and anything else that they were not able to do themselves with rubbish or in their back gardens.

I set about writing an attractive ad and placed it under the title of 'Rubbish Clearance' in a box in the *New Forest Times* which cost £35 for two weeks. The paper has since folded. I thought my ad was different to all the other ads, but just before placing it we were talking about the prospects of it being any good. Betty, my wife, couldn't see anybody wanting rubbish taken away in this form, but my feeling was a lot of people had rubbish they would like cleared but couldn't do it themselves. And a lot of people don't have room for a skip. So, setting aside whether it was a good idea or not, the ad was placed and in the very first week a £20 job came along. It had gone extremely well for something that I didn't necessarily think would go so well, right at the beginning.

By April 1983, with more and more gardening business coming along, as the year progressed I felt it might be difficult to combine the two jobs. My son Kevin was due to leave school shortly and he was planning to go on to college. I had more regular garden jobs coming out of the clearance work ad. I stopped advertising for the rest of 1983. It was a mistake really. I guess I wasn't sure what to do with the stuff and a lot of what I cleared was domestic. I wouldn't have time to sort it all out when there was something worth saving, so I put it aside. It wasn't until the following year, January 1984 to be exact, that I decided to re-place the advertisement in a square box in the *Avon Advertiser*, and I kept the ad going all the year round. For many years to come I put in this new ad, announcing 'All gardening work undertaken' as well as 'All types of rubbish cleared including sheds, furniture, compost heaps, rubble, soil etc. Large or small amounts. Fast efficient service. Very reasonable rates.' A good business was built up from my ad. I made use of a lot of the stuff that people throw out, such as wood, which I used for burning on our fire. Like everything else, we hope to become good at things; we try our hand and as time goes by, sticking to it is the hardest part. It's easier said than done in anything that we might attempt, most of it is down to circumstances.

In July 1983, Kevin had finally left school and was able to help me more regularly during the week. I had a week off from my work and we went to stay on the borders of Derbyshire so we could visit Alton Towers, a quite well known pleasure park, excellent for children or for just walking around the lovely gardens as we did with our lovely dogs, Kim and Kirsty. Just before taking the holiday, I decided we would like another Alsatian puppy which we bought from a kennel near Romsey. We called her Kim. She liked being with Kirsty who was a little older and already trained. Kim turned out to be very good, and the dogs were very good company for each other.

Derbyshire Holiday

Me and Children - Nicola, Karen and Kevin

Karen, Nicola, Kevin and Dog

In 1983 I was offered a twice-yearly contract with the main Bournemouth Post Office, cutting their Privet hedges, which were opposite the Bournemouth Railway Station. Three years earlier, just before I left British Rail, I could not have imaged that I would go on to buy myself a truck and would be running my own business. It was another good account to have to my credit. By November 1983, I wanted to improve my poor education, in not being able to spell terribly well. With more and more work coming along I needed to invoice accounts, for weekly or monthly work carried out. Most words were perfectly simple; I hear others say to themselves, easy when you know how to spell! After much improvement, I thought it would be a good idea to write this story, which has taken me two years to do.

1984-5

1984 saw the restart of the clearance work, which again brought me in new gardening jobs. In lots of cases it was just cutting hedges which had grown too high and, as always, many people never know who to ask even when there are plenty of people advertising. So word of mouth proved very fruitful. One good job came out of the clearance work and that was weekly garden maintenance at a rest home, followed by two others later that year. With the gardening side of the business quiet, as always at this time of year, it was a good job that I had thought of something new, and in addition, the wool shop wasn't going so well.

In the New Year of 1984, I realised we needed a lot more money than what we or I had hoped for in order to put the shop on a sounder financial footing once more. Regrettably, I agreed to a further advance. I was fully committed to my own side of the business, but I didn't really properly follow through with where the money was going for the shop. I needed quick access to cash to buy in new stock which didn't come when it was needed. There was a loss of trade as a silly mix-up over the application forms delayed things which meant that by the time the advance came through, we discovered it wasn't enough to pull us out of the difficulties the shop was enduring. I felt that the lack of communication between us, as to what was going on within the business, cost me a small fortune personally, which would never be returned. This is how I saw it at the time.

By April 1984, Spring was upon us and there was unusually warm and sunny weather at the time of year, and during the Summer to follow. It marked the end of my wife's dream of doing what she wanted. With my own experiences of financial difficulties, I sometimes wondered in her case, whether it was a lack of understanding, or lack of forcefulness in the end, or just bad luck, with the hot summers. Or maybe it was just the way we behaved towards one another; having more than one business in one household can cause great difficulties within itself, along with trying to keep the financial side of both straight at all times. The only advice given by the banks and accountants was to just give the business away – better to do that than go on losing money like we were. In my view regarding banks, as I already mentioned earlier, their advice leaves a lot to be desired. So often we read about other peoples' businesses going down, after taking what might seem to be perfectly good advice. But quite often people don't take it, and in many cases, the so-called experts have been proven wrong. In many cases, who knows better than the person who is running it at the time?

In my wife's case, she decided not to take the bank's or the accountant's advice, with my agreement. She tried selling it first, with more money spent on advertising. Being a little after mid-Summer, we had some response to the advert, but no firm offers. Had we got the sum needed, we wouldn't have had such a heavy price to pay afterwards. Only one person and her daughter wanted it very much, that being my wife's cousin, but they were unable to raise the funds to buy their way in, and being advised that the good will was a little too high, they withdrew, so all hopes were dashed. In the meantime, my own business was doing well with the two businesses combined, despite the very hot weather. It was just as well for us that it was as I could see another financial burden looming, even though I put it out of mind. I hoped, like most of us, that all would be well after the business had been sold.

Another two months went by and the business was still losing money. So it was decided to offer the premises at half of the original amount to my wife's cousin and daughter, and as they were keen, they accepted. After all the preliminaries of purchasing, the business was handed over on the 9th November 1984, only a few days away from three years since we moved into the premises. Still, I guess it wasn't to be. It might have failed because of the way we were, not being able to agree on what could be sold in the shop - I don't know! It's just another lesson for me to bear. Even so I was very much for it. I think where anything involves capital, especially large sums, the backer should somehow try and not lose sight of where the money goes, especially where husbands and wives' businesses are concerned.

Towards the end of 1984, Kevin was settled in his first job and my wife took a new job later in the New Year. With 1984 at an end, I saw what could have been a big financial disaster behind me. I was glad of that. The year 1985 was a slow start for me business-wise, because of the weather being so cold. Like so many businesses that involve working outside, you have to grin and bear it until the warmer weather arrives. The same year I faced quite a few challenges with work and getting my own financial position on a better footing after the previous year's setbacks. One of the greatest challenges I undertook that year, was to drive all the way to Weymouth to lay a large patio. This involved some difficulties in getting all the supplies to where they were needed as they had to be wheeled down the long narrow slope of a drive and then up a flight of steps. All the 2 by 2 slabs had to be carried up one by one to the top. An even bigger challenge as this was my first undertaking, although I'd had previous building experience. It was a challenge getting the patio slabs needed to the slope, gently, with it being so steep. With Kevin's help it was one of the greatest achievements I had taken on so far in the five years since I started the business.

I would imagine to others that it seemed like I turned up like clockwork. I always turn up near the time that I specify, or even if I ran late, I still keep going until the work is done. Most people wouldn't know that I could be covering something like 30 to 40 places per week at peak season, most of the time doing the work by myself. With the two businesses combined, it takes a lot of energy to keep going. Being the type of person that gets a bit bored very easily, it's just as well that I have more than plenty to do.

The nicest thing was when my wonderful children came with me in their holidays or on Saturdays, and if my work was near the sea, as it turned out to be quite often, we would always go to the seafront for a while, which we all liked. Having a week off in August, with my wife and three children and our lovely two Alsatians, Kim and Kirsty, I drove my lovely Ford Granada and camping trailer all the way up to a lovely part of the country in Yorkshire. We arrived early in the morning, stopped for a rest and let the dogs run about, before finding a campsite for a week's stay. Luckily, we found one by the river with lots of lovely birds and wildlife.

Having become very interested in photography, and having recently bought my first ever expensive Canon camera, costing me £500, I thought it would be a good idea to join Ringwood Camera Club. As I became good at photography, with the Camera Club's help, I began entering pictures for competitions; I managed to win a couple, with cup and a certificate. I couldn't have imagined that in future years, I would travel around the world many times with my children, and venture out by myself for what became great pictures placed in photo albums for all to see. More and more regular customers who came along enjoyed seeing my photographs of foreign visits, especially those of unusual animals.

After one week off in August it was back to work. Being a wet-ish Summer, it made things more than difficult to get around by the Autumn. My son Kevin was in his earliest years of trying out different jobs. He didn't have a job at the time and he liked the work we did. For a few weeks, he turned out to be a great help and got me over the worst of the extra work that had come my way, clearance work in particular on busy days. I regarded myself, from the time I started this business in 1980, as being very reliable and I intended to stay that way too. I turned up like clockwork, in all weathers within reason, and always will do as long as I am in this business. I had a lot energy and being the type of person I am, I never give up. Assuming that I do not give up the work I am doing at present, I hope 1986 will be as good as 1985.

Finally, to end this part of the story, on 7th November 1984, Mother died. We learned later that she had told my older brother

Brian not to tell any of us. He carried this out to the letter for the first few months after she died, but not being able to keep it to himself, eventually told my sister's friend Joan, so we soon got to hear about it, months after she had passed. Our Mother had done a good job in setting the family against one another over the years, and to make an even better job of it all, she left everything to my older brother and his children, through no fault of their own. It was so hard to comprehend that his children were the beneficiaries of all our hard work, but sadly this was the situation. It did hit me and my sister Christine very hard indeed, after all those early years of our lives and all the hard work in all weathers too, looking after all those animals we loved very much. Christine and I dreamed of having a good-sized farm one day. We did so hope for this after all our hard work. We thought there was a good chance. Of course, who wouldn't, if one worked as hard as we did. At the end of all this, my sister Christine and I felt totally let down after all our efforts. Our dream was sadly lost forever.

However, my feeling is that Mother lost out. After our final meeting in 1971, which turned sour, I realised it was no use trying to be friends ever again. A few years after this meeting, Mother bought a nice place just outside the town of Ringwood in 1979. I learned from a friend who knew Mother that she wanted to make friends. By living in the same area as we were, maybe she did. I asked myself, why didn't she contact me, if it was true? I hadn't contacted her as I didn't want the misery of being played against another member of the family, like I had been throughout my earlier years. If there was another life, all I can say, apart from some nice things that did come about, is that I wouldn't want to experience another childhood like the one I lived through. We really wondered what kind of relationship our Mother had had with her Spanish Mother who originated from Spain. We learned that Mother lost her sister through ill health, a Thyroid gland being the cause of death. Mother did tell us how awful it was for the family. She had had a private education and so did her brothers. As I saw it, and my sister Christine, she must have been terribly unhappy to keep selling up so many times and moving from one place to another, just to be close to her family members. It wasn`t the fault of me or our children. Had Mother not favoured one child or the other when it suited her, perhaps we would have had the farm she led us to believe she wanted us to have, that we had hoped for. We could have been a happy family, had she not allowed herself in turn to undermine my management of the farm.

With five years behind me in business, what are my hopes for the next five years? Perhaps I could get a bigger place? I have had an interest in rubbish almost all my life, simply because I do not like seeing rubbish strewn about the countryside. Luckily I think people are more conscious about rubbish today. I guess I started the clearance businesses at the right time. One ambition I have is to be successful in all aspects of my business, and hopefully be known and remembered for the good things I have carried out over the years, and for always trying to be helpful to all.

Kevin and Pets

Son Kevin, Me and Brother Charles

Me Gardening

Treework

Leaping Alsations at Work

Back Garden

Soraya

Karen and Oliver

Karen, Abbie and Oliver

Oliver, First Grandchild

Nicola and Sunflowers

Me and Grandson Jacob

Nicola and Jacob

Nicola and Jacob

Nicola, Jacob and Swans

Grandsons Jacob, Samuel and Isaac Wearing Original British Rail Hats

Brother Brian's Children Sarah, Paul and Sharon

Me, Kevin and Spitfire

Flying on Spitfire Day

Me at Alton Station

Me and Train

Me and Daughter Nicola Revisiting Swings at Wraysbury

Soraya at PM Ted Heath's Cathedral Close Garden in Salisbury

THE END.

Lightning Source UK Ltd.
Milton Keynes UK
UKHW041235240322
400554UK00001B/72